KEYGUIDE TO INFORMATION SOURCES ON THE
International Protection of Human Rights

KEYGUIDE TO INFORMATION SOURCES ON THE

International Protection of Human Rights

J. A. Andrews and W. D. Hines

Facts On File Publications
New York, New York

Keyguide to Information Sources on the International Protection of Human Rights

Copyright © 1987 by J. A. Andrews and W. D. Hines

Published in the United States of America by Facts on File, Inc.
460 Park Avenue South, New York 10016

First published in Great Britain by Mansell Publishing Limited
(A subsidiary of The H. W. Wilson Company)
6 All Saints Street, London N1 9RL

Library of Congress Cataloging-in-Publication Data

Andrews, John A.
  Keyguide to information sources on the international protection of human rights.

  Bibliography: p.
  Includes index.
  1. Human rights – Bibliography. I. Title.
K3236.A53   1987b   341.4'81   87-9068
ISBN 0-8160-1822-7

Printed in Great Britain

Contents

Part III List of selected organizations

Introduction

The idea of human rights has a long history but the rules and machinery for the international legal protection of the rights and freedoms of the individual are in large measure a post-1945 development. The several international and regional instruments for the protection of human rights have given rise to a substantial body of literature which is becoming of increasing significance, especially to lawyers but also to students of international affairs, philosophy, politics and other social disciplines.

The constitutional protection of human rights in the domestic law of states has an older history, and almost all states with written constitutions have now embodied some protection of the principal rights and liberties within the framework of their constitutions. There is a great deal of common ground in the rights which are protected under the international conventions and under the domestic law of states. That is especially true of Western states, but many third-world states also possess Bills of Rights modelled on the International Convention on Civil and Political Rights or the European Convention on Human Rights.

This *Keyguide* is intended to provide an introduction to the subject of the international and regional protection of human rights for the librarian and the student. It is also aimed to provide a volume for those who are interested in studying the comparative legal protection of human rights. However, it must be emphasized that the book is not a comprehensive work of reference on all aspects of human rights. In particular, it does not seek to provide a major listing of books on the philosophy of human rights or which detail political issues and arguments. The reader who is interested in these areas will find a number of comprehensive bibliographies and reference works listed in Part II of the *Keyguide* which will assist him.

There are several detailed bibliographies on the subject, some of which are rather out of date; but many are very useful. Unfortunately for the reader, most of them are not annotated. For the advanced researcher this is not a problem, but for the librarian, the new student or someone undertaking a comparative project for the first time, it can create serious difficulties. To help them, an introductory guide to the subject as well as its literature is included in Part I of the volume. It begins with an outline of the history of the concept of human rights and shows how the protection of civil liberties under the constitutions of states compares with the international protection of human rights. This is followed by an introduction to the various international instruments and the procedures available under them. In particular, by outlining the procedures available and the rights protected, it is hoped that students will obtain an insight into the opportunities available for a comparative study of the international and regional instruments and the protections existing under their own domestic law. The opportunity to make comparative references to the literature of the many international organizations operating in the field of human rights is particularly important. The work of the United Nations is central, but the developing case law under the European Convention on Human Rights offers perhaps the most interesting comparative material for the lawyer.

In Part II a fairly detailed referencing system to the international source material of human rights is provided, both in respect of treaties and other international instruments and of the developing case law. In general, the survey of secondary literature is confined to English language material, but the annotated list of monographs and textbooks contains most of the important English language works and the major reference volumes. Finally, in Part III are listed those governmental and non-governmental international organizations which have a major involvement in the legal protection of human rights.

In the preparation of the volume, we have benefited from the advice and support of Colin Hutchens on behalf of the publishers. We would like to express our appreciation to him. We are particularly grateful to the secretaries who have coped ably with tapes and manuscripts which have often been far from easy to decipher and we record our very special thanks to Anne Watkin-Jones, Eileen Pryce, Christine Davies, Wendy Davies, Awen McDougall and Sioned Roberts. In addition, we would like to express our thanks to Elizabeth Andrews who has read much of the work in typescript and proof and thereby helped to avoid too many mistakes appearing in the final work.

Abbreviations

The period since 1945 has seen an enormous proliferation in the number of national and international organizations, both governmental and non-governmental, which are concerned with the protection of human rights. These organizations are often referred to in texts by an acronym or by their initials. This is also the case for some of the major conventions and treaties, and in order to assist readers a list is included of the most common abbreviations for organizations and human rights instruments which they are likely to encounter in their reading. Many reports and journal series are also often cited in abbreviated form, and a list is included of some of the titles which the researcher is likely to encounter. The listing is of necessity selective. For details of abbreviations not listed here, the reader is referred to other works such as the *Index to Legal Citations and Abbreviations* compiled by Donald Raistrick (Abingdon, Oxfordshire: Professional Books, 1981).

Organizations

AFCM	African Commission on Human and Peoples' Rights
AI	Amnesty International
BIHR	British Institute of Human Rights
ECOSOC	United Nations Economic and Social Council
EUCM	European Commission of Human Rights
EUCT	European Court of Human Rights
FIDH	Fédération Internationale des Droits de l'Homme
IACHR	Inter-American Commission of Human Rights. Also Inter-American Court of Human Rights
IACM	Inter-American Commission of Human Rights

IACT	Inter-American Court of Human Rights
ICJ	International Court of Justice. Also International Commission of Jurists
ICRC	International Committee of the Red Cross
IIHR	International Institute of Human Rights
ILO	International Labour Organization
OAS	Organization of American States
OAU	Organization of African Unity
PCIJ	Permanent Court of International Justice
UN	United Nations
UNA	United Nations Association
UNCHR	United Nations Commission on Human Rights
UNESCO	United Nations Educational, Scientific and Cultural Organization
UNGA	United Nations General Assembly
UNHCR	United Nations High Commission for Refugees
UNHRC	United Nations Human Rights Committee

Instruments

ACHR	American Convention on Human Rights
ACHPR	African Charter on Human and Peoples' Rights
ADRDM	American Declaration of the Rights and Duties of Man
AMR	American Convention on Human Rights
ECHR	European Convention on Human Rights. May also refer to European Commission of Human Rights or European Court of Human Rights
EHR	European Convention on Human Rights
ESC	European Social Charter
ICCPR, ICPR	International Covenant on Civil and Political Rights
ICES, ICESCR	International Covenant on Economic, Social and Cultural Rights
UDHR	Universal Declaration of Human Rights
UIDHR	Universal Islamic Declaration of Human Rights

Treaty Series, Reports and Journals

AJIL	*American Journal of International Law*
BFSP	*British and Foreign State Papers*
BLD	*Bulletin of Legal Developments*
BYIL, BYBIL	*British Year Book of International Law*
Cd, Cmd, Cmnd	*Command Paper*
EHRR	*European Human Rights Reports*
ELD	*European Law Digest*

ELR	*European Law Review*
ETS	*European Treaty Series*
HRLJ	*Human Rights Law Journal*
HRR	*Human Rights Review*
ICLQ	*International and Comparative Law Quarterly*
ILM	*International Legal Materials*
LNTS	*League of Nations Treaty Series*
PAIS	*Public Affairs Information Service*
UNTS	*United Nations Treaty Series*
UNYB	*United Nations Year Book*
UNYBHR	*United Nations Year Book on Human Rights*
UST	*United States Treaties*
YBECHR	*Year Book of the European Convention on Human Rights*

PART I

Overview of the international protection of human rights and its literature

1　The General Background

Introduction

The idea of fundamental human rights has a long history, but as a subject of practical importance in terms of the protection of the quality and dignity of life of individuals, it has become of greatly increased significance since the end of the World War II. Most especially this is true in Western Europe where the impact of the European Convention on Human Rights is of major significance, not least because individuals have been able to pursue rights outside the domestic courts of their own state by taking their complaints to the European Commission of Human Rights and, in some cases, beyond to the European Court of Human Rights. The result of this is that most of the literature of significance to the subject dates from the post-World War II period.

Post-1945 developments have produced a substantial number of treaty instruments [see 26–76 and 79–85], a growing European case law on human rights and a substantial body of literature of increasing significance, especially to lawyers but also to students of international affairs, philosophy, politics and other social disciplines concerned with humanitarian factors.

The adoption by the General Assembly of the United Nations of the Universal Declaration of Human Rights in 1948 [86] has been followed by several international conventions of which the most significant are the International Covenant on Economic, Social and Cultural Rights [51], and the International Covenant on Civil and Political Rights [52], signed in 1966. At the regional level, the European Convention on Human Rights or, to give it its full title, the Convention for the Protection of Human Rights and Fundamental Freedoms [62] remains the most important instrument in practice. But several other regional instruments have been signed, including the American Declaration of the Rights and Duties of Man [108], the American Convention on Human Rights [83], the African Charter of Human and Peoples' Rights [85] and the Universal Islamic Declaration of Human Rights [109]. Although these international instruments have varying procedures for the protection of human rights – some effective and some completely ineffective – and, although the emphases vary from instrument to instrument, the substance of the rights protected includes substantial common elements and, especially in the realm of civil and political rights, the developing case law of the European Convention is likely to become of increasing significance not just to the development of a European jurisprudence of human rights, but to a whole new development of an international jurisprudence on the subject. The European Convention is sometimes attacked as representing Christian–Judaic values which do not have the same relevance in other parts of the world, and some of this criticism is justified. Nevertheless, as a source of jurisprudence of human rights, it remains the single most important instrument.

Although this *Keyguide* is concerned with the international protection of human rights, most states now have laws protecting fundamental individual rights and liberties. In many cases, these laws are a part of the constitutional framework of the country [see 110–117 and 479–505]. The opportunities for comparative study of the protection of human rights within the domestic laws of states, or between the domestic law of states and the international instruments of protection are becoming of increasing interest and importance to scholars. This work provides librarians and scholars with a starting point of reference into the international structure of human rights protection. Many of the fundamental issues which currently exercise the minds of those concerned with individual civil liberties under national laws are reflected in the legal and moral problems posed in the drafting and interpretation of international human rights instruments. Major moral and social issues concerning the right to life, the right to abortion, the scope of freedom of speech in the face of political or moral extremism, reaction to terrorism, the right to join trade unions, all have their place in the case law of human rights at national and international level.

Interest in human rights is not confined to lawyers, and the literature of human rights is by no means exclusively legal. There are important philosophical and political aspects of the subject as well as its most obvious social significance [see 349–359]. Similarly, the international protection of human rights is not exclusively a matter of international treaty law, nor is it confined to the procedural protections which have been established within the framework of the United Nations and under the various regional instruments. It is a matter of major diplomatic and political concern which is reflected in the interest shown by writers on international affairs [see 360–369] and beyond that a most important part is played by many major international organizations, both governmental and private. The importance of these bodies, especially in monitoring human rights relations, should not be underestimated and many of the more important ones are listed [611–663].

However, ultimately it is the international human rights instruments which reflect how far governments are prepared to go in providing a framework for the protection of human rights and any study of the subject must have these as its primary concern.

The Theory of Human Rights

The common perception of law is of a system laying down duties in the form 'Thou shalt not. . .'. Clearly one cannot convey the total content of law by this one concept. There are rules which prescribe the procedures and forms necessary to establish institutions, status, relationships, consequences, etc. in law. Similarly, there is adjectival or procedural law which establishes the internal content of the judicial system itself. Rules establishing the jurisdiction of courts, prescribing the procedures whereby complainants can obtain remedies, and giving force to the judgments of courts are essential to an ordered legal system.

Most law can be expressed in terms of duties together with prescriptive and procedural rules, but many other concepts are necessary for a proper analysis of the content of law and among these is the idea of rights. For our purposes, rights can be observed at two levels. In one sense they are the creatures of the law itself, depending for their existence on statute law or judge-made case law. They can be seen as a natural correlative of duties. So the rule 'Thou shalt not kill' may be seen as giving rise to the right not to be killed. The rights of the individual are established by law and remain only in so far as the law itself is not changed.

But beyond this lies a higher idea. If the only rights of man are those that are created by his legislators, then ultimately the legislators can dictate the extent of those rights. The quality of these rights may vary according to ethnic, religious, cultural and political prejudices of the moment, and minority groups, whether they be untouchable *Haryanis* of India, North American Indians, illegitimate children, Soviet Jews, or any other group which is at risk, may be disadvantaged. Indeed, entire societies may be sacrificed in the face of unreasoned dictatorship.

The argument that beyond man's law is a higher law, whether of divine, natural or ideological origin, is perhaps as old as the thinking of man himself. It has found expression in the writings of ancient Greece and Rome and of medieval and Renaissance Europe. Within this philosophical heritage is contained the thought that some rights of man are so fundamental that they are reflected in a higher order which is above the authority and responsibility of the law-maker, be he prince, governor or a democratic legislature. Some two thousand years after Sophocles had expressed the idea that the dictates of kings could not prevail over the immortal and recorded laws of the Gods, in 17th-century England one can find Lord Chief Justice Coke in *Bonham's* case saying:

When an Act of Parliament is against common right or reason or repugnant or impossible to be performed, the common law will control it, and adjudge such act to be void.

However, the practical reality is that, in the three and a half centuries which have elapsed since *Bonham's* case, the English courts have never judged an Act of Parliament to be void. For all the claim Britain has to have led the modern world in the example of democratic legislature, the complete and utter sovereignty of the United Kingdom Parliament is a cornerstone of the British legal system. (*Cf.* the views of Lord Scarman [500].)

The Constitutional Protection of Human Rights

The dignity and rights of man, a dominant theme in the political philosophy of the 18th century, flowered into practical significance with such instruments as the Virginia Declaration of Rights 1776, the American Declaration of Independence 1776, the French Declaration of the Rights of Man and of the Citizen 1789 and, of more lasting importance, the series of Amendments to the United States Constitution adopted in 1791 as the American Bill of Rights.

The constitutional settlement in the United States and the attached Bill of Rights provided a model for the protection of human rights. For many years this US model stood almost alone, but now the overwhelming majority of world states have a written constitution providing checks and balances against the abuse of authority and enshrining in one form or another fundamental rights and liberties of individuals. There is no one model. In some states the fundamental rights and liberties are protected within the Constitution itself. In other states a Bill of Rights is annexed to the Constitution subject to the same overriding primacy as the Constitution itself. In yet other states, fundamental rights are guaranteed by a Basic Law, falling short of the constitution itself but remaining paramount over the ordinary legislation of the state.

The United Kingdom remains an exception to this rule and this has generated a considerable degree of literature, not only on the issue of whether it should ever enact a modern bill of rights, but on whether it is possible constitutionally for any meaningful instrument to be enacted given the nature of the UK constitutional settlement reposing unqualified legal sovereignty in Parliament [see especially 492].

It has to be remembered that the effectiveness of the protection of human rights is dependent only in part on the rights and liberties set out in the relevant law. There are many instances of states whose constitutions contain an impressive series of human rights provisions which are not observed in practice. (See Veenhoven's 5-volume study [505] and Ashworth [551–552]). In such cases, outside pressure by international organizations, both private and public, and the existence of binding international treaty obligations are of particular importance, as is the diplomatic pressure of other states where they are willing and able to exercise it.

It is beyond the scope of this *Keyguide* to give details of individual constitutions and the human rights protections which they afford. However, the researcher should be aware of two valuable collections which are readily available in most university libraries. Amos and Dorothy Peaslee's *Constitutions of Nations* [112] provides the text in English of the constitutions of all sovereign states in a 4-volume work which is periodically updated. *Constitutions of the Countries of the World*, edited by Blaustein and Flanz [110], is issued in looseleaf form for updating and provides English translations of constitutions alongside a brief history of the constitutional development of each country. A companion series, *Constitutions of Dependencies and Special Sovereignties* [111], is also available. There are several more general works which provide selected texts and commentary [see 113–117 and 479–505].

The Content of Fundamental Human Rights

Although the principle of the fundamental rights of man finds its seed in natural law theory, there is no universal agreement on the content of human rights. The Anglo-Saxon approach has traditionally emphasized civil and political liberties of individuals alongside traditional rights to life and property and this can be seen as part of a broad Western European idea. But arguably it is morally repugnant to place civil and political rights above economic and social ones. What value is to be put on political liberty associated with a life of social and economic destitution? This issue reflects in many respects the sharp divide between East and West in today's world. Whilst the Western idea of human rights tends to stress the dignity and personality of the individual with emphases on liberty, freedom from arbitrary and excessive authority, and property rights, this is in clear contrast to socialist emphasis on economic and social rights in the context of an overall political philosophy emphasizing the significance of the collective will rather than the individual will (see *e.g.* Thompson's work [503]). Islam again stresses service to the community rather than the primacy of the individual. Property belongs to Allah and the earthly owner must use it for the benefit of the community [see 470–472].

In part, the content of the human rights idea changes as the circumstances of man change, and some writers have seen a pattern in the development of our perception of fundamental rights. This is reflected in the writings of Karel Vasak, many of which are not available in English, but see *The International Dimensions of Human Rights* [423]. One thesis advanced by R. P. Claude [484] sees the first stage in the development of human rights protection as pressure for individual and political security in the face of threats of arbitrary treatment and oppression. It is summed up by the English philosopher John Locke,

Political freedom is not being subject to the inconsistent, uncertain, unknown, arbitrary will of another man.

It means setting limits to the authority of kings and princes and ensuring that the individual shall be secure in his own family, private in his religion, and protected in his property. The basic rights associated with this stage of development are those of life, liberty and property.

If the first stage of the development is set largely in 17th- and 18th-century European thought, the second stage is clearly associated with economic and political advancement in society and with middle-class ambitions going beyond the security of property to include clear standards of justice, freedom of trade and expression. In the third stage, working classes and other deprived minority groups seek their own rights. These include freedom of assembly, wider suffrage, and the absence of discrimination against, for example, non-propertied classes, racial minorities, illegitimate children, women.

A fourth stage involves the search for positive socio-economic rights. Frequently this is prompted by the destructive effects of industrialization and colonization. Societies held together by tribalism and feudalism have the merits of protective relationships even if they do not accord with our ideas of freedom. In modern societies, old age, unemployment, sickness, unexpected destitution, and lack of educational skills often lead to serious deprivation. So at its highest level of development, the content of the human rights idea is extended to include education, medical care, social security provision, employment, etc. But, whilst many governments in developed and in developing countries have made enormous strides in providing facilities for education and health care, most have baulked at enshrining these as fundamental human rights.

For millions of people in the under-developed countries of the world, lacking food, water, shelter, medicine and the fundamental means to survive, talk of any form of human rights in the senses in which the term has been used here is irrelevant. Here the emphasis is not on freedom but on survival, and a number of modern writers have laid emphasis on a new generation of so-called development rights. In the writings of Karel Vasak [see 423], 'third generation' rights assume considerable importance. In this terminology the first generation of human rights includes the traditional civil and political protections which in large part call for a negative obligation on governments to desist from interfering with the exercise of individual liberties. The second generation of rights contains the more recently recognized economic, social and cultural rights which place a more positive duty on governments to act in order to ensure the realization of these rights. The third generation of rights is much more significantly international in content with its emphasis on solidarity. These might be taken to include rights of development for the under-developed parts of the world, rights of self-determination of peoples, their right to sovereignty over the natural resources of their country, the right to peace and the right to control one's environment. These third-generation rights are more easily associated with societies, collectivities and states than with individuals and, by and large, they form a much less significant part of the content of international treaties protecting human rights and of the literature of human rights. But there is a significant emphasis on the subject in the African Charter on Human and Peoples' Rights and in the International Covenant on Economic, Social and Cultural Rights and a growing body of literature [see 540–550].

2 International and Regional Protection

The International Treaty Protection of Human Rights

The phenomenon of international treaties protecting human rights is modern. Historically, there are illustrations of states interfering in the affairs of other states in order to protect the human rights of their own nationals or other minority groups, but often these are an aspect of a wider political imperialism which would now be contrary to Article 2(4) of the United Nations Charter which prohibits the use of force 'against the territorial integrity or political independence of any state, or in any other manner inconsistent with the Purposes of the United Nations'. More important for our purposes are the origins of a genuine international will to protect common humanitarian interests. Initially, expressions of humanitarian concern were associated with particular issues.

Slavery

Among illustrations of genuine expressions of humanitarian concern in the 19th century, the most obvious are the series of international attempts to abolish the slave trade which were to culminate in the International Slavery Convention of 1926 [23 and see also 41].

Victims of war

There were successive attempts to ameliorate the conditions of the victims of war by a series of conventions from 1864 to 1949. Beginning with a treaty which sought to ameliorate the conditions of those wounded in time of war, the protection has come to be extended to prisoners-of-war and civilians. The principal conventions are listed below [30–33 and see also 57 and 58]. To these should be added the Genocide Convention [28]. It is a depressing fact that of the 160 or so states in the world, only 96 have ratified the Genocide Convention. These include the USSR, UK, France and both Germanies, but not the USA.

Labour protection

Before the end of the 19th century there were international moves to protect conditions of work. Two conventions of a limited nature were agreed in 1906, one controlling the employment of women by night and the other the use of phosphorus in the manufacturing process. But the principal development was the establishment of the International Labour Organization [19]. Over the years, this organization has produced a series of conventions on such matters as forced labour, the right to organize and to collective bargaining and the eliminating of discrimination in employment [see *e.g.* 22, 24, 27, 29, 35, 37, 44, 47, 49, 55 and 59]. The UK, USSR and a large number of other states have ratified ILO Conventions, but the USA is a conspicuous absentee. There is a significant literature on this subject [see 506–520].

Protection of minorities

The struggle of various religious, ethnic and racial minorities to establish their independence in Central and Eastern Europe and in the Middle East were prominent factors in the war of 1914–1918. Some of the peace treaties at the war's end contained terms protecting the rights of linguistic, religious and racial minorities. The emphases in the treaties were on the right to life and liberty; the free exercise of religion without discrimination on grounds of race, religion or language; equality before the law in regard to civil and political rights; freedom to organize educational programmes and an obligation to ensure that elementary instruction of children was in their own language whenever they represented a significant minority of the population. Arbitration procedures were established and individuals were given direct access to the arbitral tribunals. The League of Nations itself became a guarantor of these protections, and states themselves could bring allegations of violations of the treaty protection to the Council of the League of Nations and in many cases claims were taken to the Permanent Court of International Justice [see 118 and 121]. Similar attempts were made to protect the rights of minorities in post-World War II peace treaties concluded with Hungary, Rumania and Bulgaria in 1947, but the procedures under these treaties have largely failed. Minorities are now protected under all the major human rights treaties by obligations not to discriminate against individuals. The major books on these treaties deal with issues of discrimination. But, in addition to that literature, there are a number of works wholly concerned with minority rights [see 551–556].

The Protection of Human Rights under the United Nations

The opening preamble of the United Nations Charter [26] expressed the purposes of the United Nations as including 'promoting and encouraging respect for human rights and for fundamental freedoms of all without distinction as to race, sex, language or religion'. Article 55 shows the responsibilities of the United Nations going well beyond the protection of civil and political rights in the classical Western tradition. It reads:

> With a view to the creation of conditions of stability and well-being which are necessary for peaceful and friendly relations among nations based on respect for the principle of equal rights and self-determination of peoples, the United Nations shall promote:
> (a) higher standards of living, full employment, and conditions of economic and social progress and development;
> (b) solutions of international economic, social, health, and related problems; and international cultural and educational co-operation; and
> (c) universal respect for, and observance of, human rights and fundamental freedoms for all without distinction as to race, sex, language, or religion.

The UN has produced an enormous amount of literature, much of which is poorly organized, but there are several guides, bibliographies and checklists to its publications [see 138–148].

Universal Declaration of Human Rights

The UN Commission on Human Rights [623] was established by the Economic and Social Council [626] of the United Nations in 1946 and its first task was to prepare an appropriate statement of human rights. This statement, the Universal Declaration of Human Rights [86], was adopted by the General Assembly of the United Nations in 1948. It remains the seminal document of the post-war period, although it is not a legally binding instrument and it was not drafted as such. It includes rights which have only limited legal substance in international law, such as the right to asylum, and it is more a statement of principle than a treaty. It was said at the time to have a moral value and authority without precedent in the history of the world. Its emphasis is very much on civil and political rights rather than economic and social rights.

UN Commission on Human Rights

Initially it was intended that the UN Commission on Human Rights would have no power to take action in respect of individual complaints of human rights violations, but since 1967 it has been authorized by the Economic and Social Council to make 'a thorough study of situations which reveal a consistent pattern of violations of human rights' and it is instructed to report its recommendations on these violations to the Economic and Social Council. The result is that the Commission has pursued a more active role in response to complaints brought to its attention by states and in response to individual petitions. *The Report of the Commission on Human Rights* is published annually [159] and is included in the Economic and Social Council Records [152]. Several other United Nations bodies work in the field [see 624–630].

The United Nations *Yearbook on Human Rights* [170] is in many ways the most valuable publication in the field. It includes the most important material in an accessible form but, unfortunately, it is very slow to appear. The *Yearbook of the United Nations* [169] summarizes major developments in this area, again with some delay in publication, while the *Bulletin of Human Rights* [151] offers a much more up-to-date account of current developments. The range of UN serial publications is very considerable and listed are those which may be of interest to the human rights student [see 150–170].

For more readable official monographs, the reader is referred to *United Nations Action in the Field of Human Rights* [173] and *United Nations and Human Rights* [174]. The general literature on the United Nations' work in the field of human rights is considerable and the principal volumes are listed in Part II [see 424–439].

The International Covenants of 1966

Following the adoption by the General Assembly of the Universal Declaration of Human Rights, the Commission on Human Rights together with the Third Committee of the General Assembly began work on a more principled and technical text which was intended to form the basis of binding treaty obligations. Eventually from this work two independent treaties emerged together with a further protocol. These were adopted by the General Assembly in 1966 as:

International Covenant on Economic, Social and Cultural Rights [51]
International Covenant on Civil and Political Rights [52]
Optional Protocol to the latter document [53]

The contrast between the International Covenant on Economic, Social and Cultural Rights and the International Covenant on Civil and Political Rights is sharp. Although it would be superficial to say they represent the East–West divide, undoubtedly they reflect the varying emphases on economic and social provision on the one hand and on civil and political freedom on the other.

The International Covenant on Economic, Social and Cultural Rights represents a substantial development in respect of human rights, although its language is much more the language of recognition than of obligation. There is only limited machinery supporting the Covenant which is largely based on the obligation of states to submit reports on the measures they have adopted under it. These reports go to the Secretary-General of the United Nations and are forwarded to the Economic and Social Council for consideration.

The International Covenant on Civil and Political Rights is a more specific document. The rights contained within it are more precisely worded and the principle of obligation is more firmly specified. Its provisions show a close similarity to the European Convention on Human Rights. Under Part IV of the Convention is established a Human Rights Committee. The basic method of enforcing the Covenant is, as with the International Covenant on Economic, Social and Cultural Rights, by submission of reports from states which go the Human Rights Committee. But under Article 41 there is an optional procedure whereby a state may declare that it recognizes the competence of the Human Rights Committee to receive communications from other states alleging that it is not fulfilling its obligations under the present Covenant. The procedure is an elaborate one and the Committee operates in secret.

Under the Optional Protocol, a state may recognize the competence of the Human Rights Committee to receive communications from individuals claiming to be victims of violations of the Convention. This is an emasculated version of the substantially more effective procedures available under the European Convention on Human Rights. The Human Rights Committee again sits in private and there is no public determination of the issue on a judicial basis.

Other United Nations instruments

The International Covenants are the major UN instruments but there are many UN General Assembly Declarations and other instruments which are of major significance: these are listed in Part II [86–106].

Other International Treaties Protecting Human Rights

Many treaties have been concluded with the protection of human rights as their prime concern or as a point of secondary emphasis. These are listed in Part II [see 17–85]. Several of these are of a specialist nature such as the Convention on the Reduction of Statelessness 1961 [46] or the European Convention on the Status of Children Born out of Wedlock 1975 [72]. Some treaties are genuinely international such as the Convention on the Elimination of All Forms of Discrimination against Women adopted by the General Assembly of the United Nations in 1979 [60] and others of a regional character such as the Convention for the Protection of Individuals with regard to Automatic Processing of Personal Data adopted by the Council of Europe in 1981 [73]. It is beyond the compass of this introduction to survey specific treaties seeking to protect human rights. There are many of them and in some cases the specific sections protecting human rights are only incidental to the main purpose of the treaty. In other cases, it would be a debatable point whether the object of the treaty could really be said to come within the parameters of the protection of human rights.

It must also be remembered that treaties are only binding on those states which have ratified them and even then some ratifying states will have made important qualifying reservations. In the listing of treaties the number of parties as at 1 January 1986 are noted. The International Court of Justice has very limited jurisdiction over states and many treaty provisions are entirely dependant on the willingness of states to fulfil their obligations.

One instrument which at the time was seen to be of great significance in the protection of human rights is the so-called Helsinki Agreement or, as it is more formally known, the Final Act of the Conference on Security and Co-operation in Europe in Helsinki of August 1975 [107]. The Final Act contains a statement of principles under the heading 'Questions Relating to Security in Europe' and was signed by 35 states including the USA and the USSR. In Chapters 7 and 8, it contains important statements in regard to human rights and fundamental freedoms and in regard to equal rights and self-determination of peoples. However, it is not a binding treaty and there is a specific provision in the agreement that it is not registerable with the Secretary-General of the United Nations which is essential if a treaty is to be evoked before any organ of the United Nations, including the International Court of Justice. To date, there is little evidence that the Helsinki Agreement has had much significance in the protection of human rights. Despite this, a considerable body of literature has been devoted to it [see 473–478].

Various index series exist to provide access to the vast range of treaties and agreements concluded between different nations. Several compendiums, each with their own indexes, are listed below [11–16], but it is also worth noting other index works. The most comprehensive guide to treaties of the 20th century, or at least those deposited with the United Nations, is provided by the *World Treaty Index*, compiled by Peter H. Rohn [15], and now in its second edition. This provides brief factual information about treaties concluded between 1900 and the early 1980s and provides reference to the particular volume, usually in the *League of Nations Treaty Series* [2] or *United Nations Treaty Series* [3], where the text of the treaty may be found. A full listing of United Kingdom treaties, both bilateral and multilateral, concluded between 1101 and 1968 was provided by Clive Parry in a 3-volume work entitled *An Index of British Treaties* [14], but this was produced in 1970 and at least as regards human rights is now somewhat dated. Access to the more important treaties is provided by a recent book by Bowman and Harris entitled *Multilateral Treaties: Index and current status* [11]. This is particularly useful since it provides a subject access to the major treaties in the area of human rights. It gives details of the dates of the various conventions, parties to agreements as at June 1983, and a variety of sources for the individual documents, including the *United Nations Treaty Series* [3], *British and Foreign State Papers* [4] and UK Parliamentary Command Paper references. The work also lists some of the regional conventions which are not found in the *World Treaty Index*. A supplementary volume provides updating to the end of 1985.

Passing reference to a few human rights instruments and conventions which are not covered by Bowman and Harris is made in a guide entitled *Current International Treaties* which was edited by T. B. Millar [13]. This is a very general work, designed to give the texts of certain major world treaties and instruments. It includes the text of the Universal Declaration of Human Rights and the two major international covenants, but only notes other instruments. Paul Sieghart's book entitled *The Lawful Rights of Mankind* [386] also gives brief details of the major international instruments, including the number of signatories as at January 1984. More recent information on the signatories and ratifications of European treaties is provided in an annual Council of Europe publication entitled *Chart Showing Signatories and Ratifications of Council of Europe Conventions and Agreements* [16]. The most recent edition is dated June 1986.

The major treaty collections, both international and regional, are listed in Part II [1–10]. Official sources are generally to be preferred in that they provide the authoritative text of the relevant agreement. However, it must be emphasized that a variety of commerically produced journals provide documentation which is perfectly acceptable for most students. Although references to texts in collections such as the *United Nations Treaty Series* [3] are generally provided, alternative sources such as *International Legal Materials* [275] or the *American Journal of International Law* [247] may also be of value, especially since they often provide more up-to-date coverage than is to be found in the official series. Instruments other than conventions, such as declarations or UN General Assembly resolutions, may be more difficult to obtain, although reference is provided to one useful collection produced by Djonovich [7]. The coverage of such instruments is necessarily selective, although the more significant items have been included [86–106].

Regional Arrangements for the Protection of Human Rights

European Convention on Human Rights

The European Convention has been ratified by all 21 member states of the Council of Europe. Its emphasis is on the protection of civil and political rights and its content parallels the Universal Declaration of Human Rights and the International Covenant on Civil and Political Rights, though the latter was not open for signature until 1966. For students of human rights its significance goes beyond any other instrument in terms of the effectiveness of its procedures, and the literature arising from the ECHR is considerable. The bibliographic sources are unfortunately rather out of date [see 198, 200 and 210], but the serial literature, most of which is obtainable from the Directorate of Human Rights [612], is very helpful [see 202–212]. The *Yearbook of the ECHR* [213] is published commercially, but again is a valuable work of reference. The more significant monograph literature is listed separately [see 440–463].

The Convention establishes a European Commission of Human Rights and a European Court of Human Rights. There are several books discussing the procedures whereby the European Convention is enforced [see *e.g.* 441, 444, 446, 452 and 454] and it is these procedures for enforcement, together with the developing case law of the European Court and Commission, which make this Convention so significant in the study of international human rights law protection.

The Commission can deal with allegations of breaches of the Convention referred to them by states which are parties to it and, most important of all, it can hear applications by individuals against those states which have made a specific declaration under Article 25 of the Covenant declaring that they accept the right of individual petition. At the present time all but four states have made this declaration. By the end of 1985 the Commission had received 31,146 applications and petitions which were provisionally filed although many of them were not followed up. 450 applications have been declared admissible and the Commission has investigated the applications on their merits.

There are a number of reasons why many petitions fail to satisfy the test of admissibility. In some cases the petitioner does not disclose sufficient information for his case to get off the ground and, indeed, the Commission has now adopted a procedure whereby such correspondence is given a provisional file, but is not officially recorded as an application until sufficient details are received. So far 11,891 applications have been registered out of the 31,146 provisional complaints received. This change in procedure, which took place in 1973, needs to be borne in mind in any study of the statistics of petitions.

But even where sufficient preliminary information is given for the petition to be recorded, there are a number of hurdles which have to be overcome. Some petitions fail because they are brought against states that are not parties to the Convention, or they concern rights which are not themselves protected under the Convention, or they are clearly an abuse of the Convention, or the petitioner has not exhausted his local remedies.

The opinions of the Commission in regard to cases where it has heard argument on the merits are clearly of considerable importance in the development of the Convention, but to some extent so are its decisions on admissibility, many of which are published. These provide a substantial repository of information showing the limitations on the application of the Convention and are an important source of reference. Opinions of the Commission on the merits of individual applications and decisions on admissibility are published in *Decisions and Reports* [129], and formerly in *Collections of Decisions* [128], and in the *European Human Rights Reports* [see 137]. The range of periodical material relating to decisions of the Commission is listed in Part II [128–131].

Over and beyond the right of individual petition to the Commission was the equally revolutionary provision to establish a Court whose decisions are binding on the states which are parties to the Convention, provided that they have made an appropriate declaration under Article 46 accepting the compulsory jurisdiction of the Court. At present, all but two of the parties to the Convention accept this compulsory jurisdiction.

After the Commission has given its opinion on the merits of a case, it is open to the Commission itself or to the state against whom the complaint has been made or to the state making the complaint or to a state whose national is alleged to be the victim of a violation of the Convention to bring the case before the European Court of Human Rights. It is the judgments of the Court which, more than anything else, develop the jurisprudence of human rights under the European

Convention. No other international instrument for the protection of human rights has produced a body of case law which is in any way comparable. All decisions of the Court are reported [see 125–127].

The states which are parties to the Convention undertake to secure to everyone within their jurisdiction the rights and freedoms of the Convention, and many European states have incorporated it into their domestic law. For some of these states the decisions of the Court can have a direct bearing and can be cited in argument in their domestic courts. Even for those states which have not incorporated the Convention, the decisions of the Court are of considerable importance and, where the Court finds a violation of the Convention, it will often lead to legislation bringing domestic law into line with the state's treaty obligations.

The European Convention itself has been developed by a series of additional Protocols of which currently there are eight [see 63, 67–70 and 74–76]. Five of these are concerned with procedural amendments whilst the others have added additional rights to the list of those already protected.

European Social Charter
The European Convention on Human Rights confines itself to civil and political rights, although the First Protocol does include somewhat circumscribed provisions in regard to the right to education. A complementary European Social Charter [66] was opened for signature in 1961, but only 14 states have ratified it and two of the 21 members of the Council of Europe have not even signed it. In some ways it parallels the International Covenant on Economic, Social and Cultural Rights, signed in 1966. The literature on the European Social Charter is much less than that on the ECHR, but a *Bibliography* was published in 1982 [199] and the recently published book by D. Harris, *The European Social Charter* [448], has made its study much easier.

American Declaration of the Rights and Duties of Man
The Organization of American States adopted the American Declaration of the Rights and Duties of Man in 1948 [108]. Its language is very reminiscent of the Universal Declaration of Human Rights [86] adopted by the General Assembly of the UN in that same year and it is not a binding treaty. Nevertheless the Inter-American Commission on Human Rights was established in 1959 by the Declaration of Santiago and charged with the responsibility of promoting respect for human rights within the Organization of American States. All 27 members of the Organization of American States including the USA have signed the American Declaration of the Rights and Duties of Man.

The overall position in regard to the protection of human rights under the Charter of the Organization of American States is somewhat confusing, not least because of the overlapping relationship of the Inter-American Commission on Human Rights which has functions both in regard to the more substantial American Convention on Human Rights and in regard to the American Declaration of the Rights and Duties of Man. There is a small and important body of literature on this subject [see *e.g.* 468 and 469] which could be particularly significant in the case of the USA which was a party to the Declaration, but has not ratified the Convention.

American Convention of Human Rights

The American Convention on Human Rights [83] was signed in Costa Rica in 1969 by the member states of the Organization of American States and entered into force in 1978 after receiving the appropriate ratifications. At the present time, 19 states have ratified the Convention, the most obvious absentees being the USA and Canada. Canada is not a member of the Organization of American States. The failure of the USA to ratify the Convention has remained a severe disappointment.

Those who framed the American Convention on Human Rights drew substantially from the wording of the European Convention and from the International Covenant on Civil and Political Rights. They were also able to draw from the procedural experiences under the European Convention, though in 1969 these were more limited than they are today. The American Convention, like the European Convention, provides for a Commission and a Court, but there are major procedural differences. An essential source book on the subject is *Human Rights: The Inter-American System* by Buergenthal and Norris [464] and other useful works are listed below [465–467].

Partly because so few states have recognized the binding jurisdiction of the Court, but also because of the relative recentness with which the American Convention has come into effect, there is no body of jurisprudence under the American Convention on Human Rights corresponding to that which has emerged under the European Convention, and it is likely to be many years before such a body of jurisprudence does emerge. Such cases as have fallen to be decided by the Court have come largely by virtue of its power to give advisory opinions. The most accessible sources for judgments of the Inter-American Court of Human Rights include, perhaps oddly, the *European Human Rights Reports* [137], the *Human Rights Law Journal* [265] and the *American Journal of International Law* [247]. Neither the Organization of American States nor the Inter-American Court nor Commission is anything like as helpful in correspondence as the Council of Europe and the European Court and Commission.

African Charter of Human and Peoples' Rights

Many of the newly independent African countries include within their constitutional framework provisions protecting human rights and fundamental freedoms. In some cases these are embodied directly within their constitution and in others they are annexed as a separate instrument. In many cases these protections are modelled on the European Convention on Human Rights or derived from the General Assembly's Universal Declaration.

The continent of Africa includes at least 20 of the 30 poorest countries in the world and it is arguable that the freedoms and privileges of developed European society are not immediately relevant to the quality of life in a country where the greatest threat is drought or disease. Nevertheless, with major problems of tribal and religious discrimination, political authoritarianism, military coups, the systematic persecution of minorities and the impermanence of existing governments, many African countries have a strong need to establish a framework for the protection of human rights.

The African Charter of Human and Peoples' Rights [85] was approved in 1981 and sensibly represents a compromise between the need to protect the interests of the individual on the one hand and to ensure that they do not conflict with the need for comprehensive social and economic development plans by the state on the other. In a unique and significant way, the Charter seeks to fuse the idea of rights and duties of individuals.

Although the document is called a Charter, it takes a similar form to the European and American Conventions. It is not yet in force, having not received the required number of ratifications. As of 1 January 1986, 17 states had ratified the Charter and a further 7 had signed but not ratified; it needs 26 ratifications to come into force. Undoubtedly some states will find difficulty in ratifying a document, some of whose articles are closely modelled on the European pattern.

There is no equivalent of the European Court of Human Rights, but under the Charter a Commission is established which has responsibility to promote and protect human and peoples' rights and to interpret the provisions of the Charter. There is machinery for the referring of violations or allegations of violations of human rights to the Commission.

In an interesting and novel way, the African Charter provides that the Commission should 'draw inspiration from international law on human and peoples' rights' and refers particularly to the various African and United Nations instruments in the field of human rights. It also directs the Commission to take into consideration, as subsidiary measures to determine the principles of law applicable, other general or special international conventions, provided they are consistent with international norms on human and peoples' rights, together with international customs generally accepted as law, and with the general principles of law recognized by African states.

Universal Islamic Declaration of Human Rights

The Universal Islamic Declaration [109] was signed at a meeting of the Islamic Council in September 1981. It is a different instrument from the regional conventions and charters and nearer in authority to the Universal Declaration of the General Assembly or the American Declaration of the Rights and Duties of Man. Its principal value to students is as a comparative instrument to compare with the regional conventions and the UN covenants. The common factor which brings its signatories together is religious rather than regional of course, and it draws justification and authority from reference to the Holy Qur'an and the Sunnah. However, many of its provisions show coincidence with those of the other major human rights instruments. It contains references to the right to life, to freedom under the law, to equality before the law, to fair trial, to freedom from torture and many other matters which will be found in the conventions. But, particularly within its Preamble, there are expressed a number of principles which have profound socio-political significance. For example, the principle is expressed that 'obedience shall be rendered only to those commands which are in consonance with the Law'. It is of course God who is the Source of all Law in the Islamic world. In that same Preamble it is stated that all worldly power is 'a sacred trust, to be exercised within the limits prescribed by the Law . . .'. It is further provided that all economic resources are to be treated as 'Divine Blessings bestowed upon mankind, to be enjoyed by all in accordance with the rules and values set out in the Qur'an and the Sunnah'. There is very little literature on the subject, but there are a few books in English on the general theme of human rights in Islam [see 470–472].

3   The Structure and Substance of Human Rights Protection

This chapter is intended primarily for students of law, politics, philosophy and other social sciences who are interested to study the international and comparative dimensions of human rights protection. Many law students and students of government, politics, etc., are primarily concerned with the study of their own national institutions. But the international and regional protection of human rights is important in two ways. First, the international and regional protection may have internal application within the state. This is especially so for many states which are parties to the European Convention on Human Rights. The subject is dealt with in A. Drzemczewski's excellent book, *European Human Rights Convention in Domestic Law: A comparative study* [444]. Secondly, it offers very considerable opportunities for comparative study. This is obvious when one realizes the extent to which the major international and regional instruments have borrowed from each other. But beyond that, many states have incorporated constitutional protections modelled on one or other of these instruments. The ECHR was used as a common model for several newly independent African states.

For students who seek to study the international, comparative aspects of the subject for the first time or who are contemplating comparative projects, this chapter offers an outline of the structure of the subject and of the principal rights protected. Rights are not absolute things; they have to be qualified in the interests of others and of society.

General Principles of Human Rights

Clearly an international instrument cannot simply list the human rights which it protects. The scope of the right must be defined. For example, what is the relationship of the basic principle of the right to life and such associated issues as the right to an abortion or suicide or to voluntary euthanasia or capital punishment? But beyond that, human rights cannot be seen in isolation. One man may wish his right to freedom of speech to allow him to libel his neighbour; his neighbour is not likely to agree. Human rights have to be interpreted with some degree of relativity to ensure fairness to all and to the interests of society as a whole. In this respect, the general principles which temper the impact of substantive human rights in their individual application are vitally important in determining the ultimate scope of human rights protection. All the major international instruments have qualifying provisions and anyone studying their provisions or seeking to claim rights under them must have regard to this fact.

The right to non-discrimination

The American Declaration of Independence of July 1776 stated unequivocably, 'We hold these truths to be self-evident, that all men are created equal . . .'. It is a tragedy of US history that the bold ideals of the founding fathers were quickly and severely qualified by political and economic realities. The ultimate discrimination – slavery of one man to another – was to endure in the United States for a further century. There are still areas of the world where severe discrimination is practised, but the modern principles of human rights outlaw most forms of distinction and discrimination. The United Nations Charter speaks of encouraging respect for human rights and fundamental freedoms 'for all without distinction as to race, sex, language or religion'. The principle is widened in Article 2 of the Universal Declaration of Human Rights to exclude 'distinction of any kind, such as race, colour, sex, language, religion, political or other opinion, national or social origin, property, birth or other status'.

This right to non-discrimination is repeated in the International Covenant on Civil and Political Rights and in the European and American Conventions. Understandably the African Charter widens it to exclude discrimination on grounds of 'ethnic group'.

Students of human rights need to bear in mind that the right to non-discrimination can serve to widen the substantive rights which are protected. So, for example, an international convention may not provide any specific rights to illegitimate children but, if a state under its own law unfairly discriminates between them and the rights it gives to legitimate children, then that state may be in violation of its obligation to ensure that the rights and freedoms enjoyed under a treaty are secured without discrimination. The way in which this works under the European Convention is that, although no provision is directly made protecting illegitimate children, the specific rights to private and family life, to property, etc. must be secured without discrimination. In so far as a state makes provision for legitimate children to rights of name, relationship, guardianship, inheritance, etc., it will not be able to discriminate against illegitimate children unless it can satisfy the Commission or Court that the discrimination is reasonable and based on objective grounds. The impact which such general principles may have on the content of specific rights is something which neither the student nor the practitioner can ignore. The obligation to avoid discrimination in respect of the rights under the Convention has provided rich opportunities to develop the jurisprudence under the ECHR. An older but still useful work on this subject is E. W. Vierdag's *The Concept of Discrimination in International Law with Special Reference to Human Rights* [392], but many of the monographs listed on the European Convention [440-463] deal with the subject. The case law is considerable and the index to the subject matter of cases reported in the *European Human Rights Reports* [137] is helpful in providing a starting point for study.

The obligation to society

There is a contrast and a potentiality for conflict between a political philosophy which emphasizes the rights of the individual and one based on the principle of the collective solidarity of society. Western European emphasis is very much on individual rights and the relative curtailment of the authority of the state, though recognizing that the rights of the individual must sometimes be limited in the interests of the state or society as a whole. Under the European Convention on Human Rights, many of the rights have qualifying provisions. Typical of this is the protection of the right to privacy, to family life and associated matters under Article 8. This Article reads:

1. Everyone has the right to respect for his private and family life, his home and his correspondence.
2. There shall be no interference by a public authority with the exercise of this right except such as is in accordance with the law and is necessary in a democratic society in the interests of national security, public safety or the economic well-being of the country, for the prevention of disorder or crime, for the protection of health or morals, or for the protection of the rights and freedoms of others.

In contrast, other Articles are stated in an unqualified form. So the text of Article 3 simply reads:

No one shall be subjected to torture or to inhuman or degrading treatment or punishment.

The different rights protected under the European Convention are drafted in varying ways and with varying levels of qualification. The American Convention on Human Rights adopts a similar pattern and it is possible to develop an argument that there is something of a hierarchy of human rights with some rights being of a rather more absolute nature than others. Clearly society could be threatened by somebody abusing his right to freedom of speech but not by its inability to subject somebody to torture. For the student or practitioner, the right cannot be divorced from its qualifications and it is important to remember that these qualifications on individual human rights are not necessarily contained within the individual articles protecting those rights. Other matters have to be taken into account, including the general principles which may govern the extent of human rights.

International instruments commonly provide that states can derogate from their obligations in respect of human rights where this is required in time of war or other public emergencies threatening the life of the state. Even here, as in the case of the European and American Conventions, certain rights are regarded as paramount and no derogation is allowed even in time of war. These include the right to life, to freedom from torture, inhuman and degrading treatment or punishment, and freedom from slavery.

Other instruments go further, underlining the collective interest of the state. Article 29(1) of the General Assembly's Universal Declaration of Human Rights states, 'Everyone has duties to the community in which alone the freedom for the development of his personality is possible'. And the American Convention, Article 32, speaks of every person having responsibilities 'to his family, his community and mankind'. The African Charter goes much further again. Article 27 talks of the individual's duties to 'his family and society, the state and other legally recognised communities and the international community', while Article 29 places a whole series of obligations upon the individual to ensure service to the national community, protection of the security of the state, the preservation and strengthening of social and national solidarity and the strengthening of African cultural values, among other aims. The ambit of the African Charter is much wider than an instrument simply seeking to protect individual civil and political rights. It is also an instrument of collective obligation.

Abuse of rights

As we have seen, it is necessary to balance the competing interests of individuals and others, including those of the community and the state, and virtually all human rights instruments do this in one way or another. The Universal Declaration speaks of everyone, in the exercise of his rights and freedoms, being subject to some degree of limitation in order to secure due recognition and respect for the rights and freedoms of others (Article 29.2).

The European Convention, Article 17, provides that it shall not be interpreted as implying for any state, group or person the right to engage in any activity aimed at the destruction of any of the rights and freedoms set forth within it, and many of the rights are so defined as to allow the state to restrict them in the interests of its own well-being and those of others. Clearly, the right of freedom of speech could not be extended to cover the right to teach racist or other subversive ideas which could be destructive of the underlying and fundamental values of society.

The margin of appreciation

To what extent should the content of human rights vary, if at all, between different communities? Clearly, where an instrument provides that a right may be limited by the state 'insofar as is necessary for the maintenance of public order or the economic well-being of the state, etc.', then the extent to which an individual state can restrict the operation of the right will vary according to different factors affecting the state's economic, social or political stability. It is natural that the scope which a state may reasonably be expected to allow for freedom of speech may vary between a stable, developed democracy and a newly independent state threatened with insurgency.

The European Convention on Human Rights has produced most of the jurisprudence on this subject and several of the principal textbooks deal with the issue. Despite their relative social and cultural harmony, member states of the Council of Europe clearly have their differences and a recurrent issue in the judgments of the European Court of Human Rights has been the extent to which European values and norms of behaviour can be regarded as having some degree of universality among the member states. If most member states have abolished corporal punishment, can its continued use by one state be regarded as inhuman or degrading treatment in violation of the Convention, even if historically that state has regarded corporal punishment as a normal phenomenon? Similarly, if most states allow homosexual activities between consenting male adults in private, will its continued proscription in one area of Western Europe be a violation of the right of an individual to respect for his private life, even though that state has regarded such proscription as a fundamental part of its moral structure? In recognizing the developing norms of behaviour and changing values in Western European society, and giving weight to these in its interpretation of the European Convention, the Court has given a dynamic to the European Convention on Human Rights which has exceeded the expectations of those who framed the instrument. It would be an exaggeration to suggest that the European Convention on Human Rights has been given a dynamic comparable with, say, the American Constitutional Amendments, but the European Convention is not yet 40 years old and already the scope of its protections has substantially exceeded the expectations of its creators. This is discussed in *The Dynamics of Development in the European Human Rights Convention System* by C. C. Morrison [456]. It makes the case law under the Convention particularly important in interpreting the current scope of the rights protected in a way which is unique for an international treaty and more comparable with the constitutional case law of states like the USA. It provides a very fertile field for scholars.

The European Court of Human Rights has developed an important doctrine in the exercise of its judicial role. Adopted from French administrative law, the concept of a 'margin of appreciation' introduces an interesting variable in the application of the Convention. Put briefly, it allows the Court to have regard, not only to the differing moral, social, economic, political and cultural considerations which affect the lives of member states in differing ways, but also to the immediate authority and responsibility of the domestic state itself in its legislative and administrative role. The doctrine has been applied with varying strengths. For example, the Court has recognized that a state must respond immediately in the face of political emergencies and must have a degree of discretion to itself in deciding whether a derogation from its obligations under the Convention is 'strictly required' by the situation. Similarly, the Court has taken the view that in its censorship of literature the state must be given some margin of discretion within which to appreciate the needs of its own society. On the other hand, the European Court has not been prepared to extend a wide discretion to the state to use its own law of contempt of court to control freedom of speech. The Court has taken the view that there is a more objectively recognized European standard of judicial responsibility, leaving less scope for state discretion in this area. The case law and the literature on this topic are still developing.

Specific Human Rights

The list of fundamental rights and liberties is not a closed one, but there is agreement on a core of individual rights and freedoms which include the right to life, liberty, freedom from slavery and from torture, inhuman and degrading treatment, together with the right to fair process of law and the central freedoms of thought, speech, religion and assembly. Other rights are less clearly established, including such matters as the right of political asylum, rights of residence and many social and economic rights. Even for those rights which are clearly accepted, there can be considerable dispute as to the scope of the right as we have noted.

Here, the principal human rights and freedoms are outlined and some introductory comments made on the principal issues surrounding them as an introduction to the developing literature on the subject.

Right to life

The right to life is the most fundamental of rights. The Genocide Convention [28] seeks to protect national, ethnic, racial or religious groups from being destroyed in whole or in part and goes beyond protecting the lives of members of such groups to include such matters as causing serious bodily or mental harm, deliberately inflicting conditions of life calculated to bring about physical destruction of the group, imposing measures to prevent births and forcibly transferring children of one group to another.

All the international and regional instruments seeking to protect civil and political rights include a provision protecting the right to life itself and most contemporary jurisprudence is concerned not with the general issue of the right, but with specific aspects of the extent to which it should be protected. There is a rapidly growing literature on the right to life versus the right to abortion issue, most of which comes from pressure groups seeking to impose their own political or moral stance on others, but there is also a significant case law under the European Convention. The same concentration on moral and social principles applies at the other end of the human life scale on such matters as the right to suicide and, more particularly, the issues surrounding the aiding and abetting of suicide, euthanasia and various aspects of treatment of terminally ill patients; and of continuing significance is the issue of capital punishment.

All these areas present serious moral, legal and social issues for the domestic law of states and it is noticeable how much case law has developed from the United States Constitutional Amendments in regard to these items. The international instruments present difficult issues of interpretation as to whether they provide a right to life for the foetus, and there is likelihood of a growing jurisprudence in this area. Most recently the Council of Europe has adopted Protocol No. 6 to the European Convention on Human Rights [74] seeking the abolition of the death penalty. The American Convention deals with the issue in its own text.

Freedom from torture, inhuman or degrading treatment or punishment

The prohibition of torture, cruel, inhuman or degrading treatment or punishment appears as an early article in the General Assembly's Universal Declaration of Human Rights. It recurs in all the other principal international and regional conventions establishing civil and political rights, and the United Nations has maintained a continuing interest in the subject. The International Covenant on Civil and Political Rights of 1966 extends the prohibition to include subjection, without free consent, to 'medical or scientific experimentation' and in 1975 the United Nations General Assembly adopted a Declaration on the Protection of All Persons from Being Subjected to Torture and Other Cruel, Inhuman or Degrading Treatment or Punishment [102].

Exactly what amounts to torture or to inhuman or degrading treatment or punishment remains a controversial issue. It has proved so in the interpretation of the European Convention on Human Rights both in regard to measures taken to interrogate suspected terrorists and in the problems which arise in holding terrorist suspects and offenders in circumstances of maximum security. The provision has important application in regard to the ability of states to impose corporal punishment on offenders. There is a significant European jurisprudence on this subject.

For a disturbing review of the use of torture today, the reader is referred to Amnesty International's *Torture in the Eighties* [571].

Freedom from slavery and servitude

The principle that all men are born free and equal is one which has found slow acceptance. Efforts to abolish the slave trade, and eventually slavery itself, provided an important forerunner of the modern movement to provide broader international protection of human rights. The principal convention remains the Slavery Convention of 1926 [23].

Forced labour can be equally as inhuman and degrading as slavery itself and, whilst the Universal Declaration of Human Rights of 1948 establishes a prohibition of slavery, servitude and the slave trade, most of the major conventions have extended the prohibition to include forced and compulsory labour. Exceptions are usually provided in the case of compulsory military service, compulsory service required in emergencies and calamities, and work or service forming part of normal civic obligations.

The African Charter approaches the problem in a different way. Slavery and the slave trade are included along with torture, inhuman treatment and punishment as matters prohibited under Article 5 of that Charter. But there is no corresponding provision in regard to forced and compulsory labour. Indeed, under Article 29 the individual's duties include the obligation to place his physical and intellectual abilities at the service of his national community. This again illustrates the emphasis on social solidarity in the African Charter.

A substantial protection of workers' rights has been established through the work of the International Labour Organization, and several of the conventions included under the auspices of that body protect the freedom and conditions of workers. There is considerable literature on the work of the ILO [see 182–194 and 506–520].

Right to liberty and security of person

The right to liberty is one of the classic political freedoms, clearly established in all the main international conventions protecting civil and political rights. The principle has a long history, but inevitably the right is circumscribed. The detention of persons convicted of crime, or remanded in custody pending trial, or detained for reasons of mental health or because they are contagiously ill, or because they are remanded in custody pending deportation, are some of the more obvious circumstances in which most states deny individuals their freedom. The result is that the significance of most of the provisions protecting the right to liberty and security of person is related to the procedures established to protect the right rather than to establishing the absoluteness of the right itself.

Historically, the common law remedy of *Habeas corpus*, which does not establish a right to liberty but rather a procedure whereby the lawfulness of detention can be challenged, has always been seen to be of great significance in protecting the individual against the arbitrariness of the executive. Modern international and regional conventions reflect this principle in providing procedures preventing arbitrary detention. Typically, the African Charter provides that no one may be deprived of his freedom except for reasons and conditions previously laid down by law. The International Covenant on Civil and Political Rights, the European Convention and the American Convention go into the subject in greater detail, listing the circumstances in which a person may be deprived of his liberty as well as ensuring that any deprivation of liberty must be in accordance with procedures prescribed by law.

The experience of the European Convention has shown that a large proportion of the petitions received by the Commission originate from persons who are either in prison or detained in some way. Many of these do not disclose a violation of the Convention and they are dismissed without a hearing on the merits. But several such cases have been admitted and a number of these have found their way to the European Court of Human Rights. This has led to the development of a substantial body of jurisprudence on the subject, and one consequence of these cases has been changes in the domestic law of several of the states which are parties to the Convention. Much of this jurisprudence under the Convention is of considerable comparative interest, since most national laws have parallel provisions seeking to protect individuals from arbitrary arrest and detention.

Right to fair, public and speedy trial

This is often associated with the right to liberty, and several of the applications which come before the European Commission on Human Rights involve issues of unlawful detention coupled with delays in the process of trial. But the underlying protections are different. The right to liberty is concerned with a person's freedom from arrest and detention and seeks to circumscribe the circumstances in which he can be detained and to confirm the procedures which are available to him to challenge the legality of that detention. The right to a fair and public trial is not necessarily associated with issues of liberty. It protects the ability of a person to have his civil rights and obligations determined fairly and publicly within a reasonable time. It also entitles him to have criminal charges against him determined in the same fair and public way in a reasonable time, irrespective of whether he is remanded in custody or faces the threat of imprisonment.

Underlying this area of law is the concept of due process of law embedded in the English Bill of Rights of 1688 and recurring as a theme in the United States Bill of Rights. There is a substantial body of jurisprudence under the European Convention associated with such issues as the independence and impartiality of tribunals, the right to public hearing and public pronouncement of judgment and, more particularly, with the various protections surrounding the trial of criminal charges. These include the presumption of innocence, the right of a defendant to be informed promptly of the charges against him and to have adequate time and facilities to prepare his defence including, where necessary, the provision of legal aid.

A right which properly stands on its own, but which is often associated with fair process of law, is that of every man not to be criminally liable for conduct which was not an offence at the time when it took place. Similarly, he should not be subject to a heavier penalty than that which was applicable at the time of his offence. This principle, enshrined in Article 7 of the European Convention, could have important consequences in the common law where the ability of judges to develop the law by interpretation does mean that particular behaviour may be perceived to be criminal only after lengthy legal argument and judicial deliberation to ascertain what the law is. As yet, there is little jurisprudence on this subject. However, several of the rights under the Convention can be limited by states in so far as is necessary in a democratic society, provided the limitation is 'in accordance with law' or 'prescribed by law', and here the European Court of Human Rights has reasoned that this requires that the rule of law within the state must be adequately accessible and formulated with sufficient precision to enable a citizen to regulate his conduct.

Right to private and family life

Most modern human rights instruments contain a right to privacy. The Universal Declaration of Human Rights set the pattern of protection by providing that no one should be subjected 'to arbitrary interference with his privacy, family, home or correspondence, nor to attacks upon his honour and reputation'. Each of these interests is protected by the American Convention and the International Covenant on Civil and Political Rights. The European Convention is more limited, confining itself to respect for private and family life, home and correspondence. The emphasis in the African Charter is very much more on the dignity of the individual than on the right to private life.

The right to privacy can conflict with the interests of the state, and the different instruments provide varying ways of qualifying the right where there is a conflict. The European Convention has a detailed provision allowing the state to interfere with the exercise of the right 'as is in accordance with the law and is necessary in a democratic society in the interests of national security, public safety or the economic well-being of the country, for the prevention of disorder or crime, for the protection of health or morals, or for the protection of the rights and freedoms of others'. An alternative approach is adopted by the American Convention which provides that each person's rights are limited by the rights of others, by the security of all, and by the just demands of the general welfare, in a democratic society. The principle is the same but the wording is more general and capable of more varied interpretation than that used in the European Convention.

In the case of the European Convention, the interpretation of the phrase 'right to private life' has raised a number of important issues. Initially the right was intended to protect the individual against excessive interference by the state and its police, including such things as forcible separation of families, arbitrary searches and interference with correspondence, and under the ECHR there is important case law on such issues as telephone tapping. But the right to private life has also been used, admittedly unsuccessfully, to argue that, among other things, municipal restrictions on the right to keep dogs and compulsory psychiatric examination for the mentally disordered violate the Convention. More positively, the right has been used to challenge the inequalities and unfairness of Belgian law regarding illegitimacy, Irish rules on legal aid which make it excessively difficult for persons to obtain judicial separation, Northern Irish rules prohibiting homosexuality between consenting male adults and, in several cases, the rules of the United Kingdom Home Office restricting prisoners' rights of correspondence. Attempts are being made to use the case law to challenge prohibitions on divorce and to force states to recognize changes of sex by individuals. At some stage, attempts will no doubt be made to use the right to private and family life to argue that states should be forced to recognize homosexual 'marriages'.

The case material of the European Court is substantial, lively and full of interest for the student and the researcher. It has some parallels with the case law in the United States Supreme Court, and there are other obvious areas of comparative interest with the case law and legislation of other states and with current areas of legal, political and moral controversy. This is a fertile field of study for the comparative lawyer.

Right to marry and found a family

This right is distinct from that to private and family life. It is concerned not so much with the integrity of the family from outside interference as with the rights of individuals to marry and to start a family. The International Covenant on Civil and Political Rights establishes the family as 'the natural and fundamental group unit of society' before stating the right of men and women of marriageable age to marry and found a family.

The American Convention requires that the parties should meet the conditions required by domestic law, but the European Convention is less restrictive. There is a substantial amount of European jurisprudence ranging over such issues as the right to marry by proxy, the right to enter and reside in another country in order to marry and set up a family, the right of prisoners to marry and the right of conjugal visits to persons in prison. Any attempt by states to introduce eugenic or racial controls over marriage would conflict with the non-discriminatory protections of the major international instruments.

Both the American and the European Convention contain a provision that no marriage shall be entered into without the free and full consent of intending spouses which strikes directly at the system of arranged marriages often practised among Asian families, unless the arrangement is made with the full, informed consent of the parties themselves. The right does not concern itself with relations between the parties.

The African Charter and the Islamic Declaration offer interesting points of contrast. The African Charter concentrates on the issue of the family, providing in Article 18 that it should be the natural unit and basis of society. It further provides that the unit should be protected by the state and, indeed, goes further to provide that the state has a duty to assist the family 'which is the custodian of morals and traditional values recognised by the community'.

The Islamic Declaration goes further, providing that every person is entitled to marry and establish a family and to bring up his children in conformity with his religion, traditions and culture. It provides among other things for the obligations of the husband to maintain his wife and children, the right of children to be maintained and properly brought up and the obligation of the community to provide for the child if the parents are unable. This right goes well beyond the mere protection of the usual Western civil and political liberties, and contains important emphases on social provision and obligation.

Freedom of thought, conscience and religion

All the main international human rights instruments protect freedoms of thought, conscience and religion. The only case law of significance under the ECHR concerns itself largely with the manifestation of religious belief. These include such issues as whether Sikhs should be entitled to wear turbans instead of school hats or should be exempt from wearing crash helmets when motor cycling, to what extent individuals are entitled to take time off work for religious observance, the extent to which teachers and others should be restricted in what they teach so as to prevent religious and other forms of indoctrination and the extent to which holders of religious offices may be barred from civil or judicial office.

The Islamic Declaration of Human Rights presents important contrasts for the comparativist. It protects the right of every person to express his thoughts and beliefs, but only in so far as he remains within the limits prescribed by the Law and, within this context, that means the Law divined from the revelations of Allah through the Holy Scriptures. The Islamic Declaration contains a careful balance. The pursuit of knowledge and the search after truth is predicated as a duty of every Moslem, but so also is respect for the religious feelings of others, and it is stated within the Declaration that 'no-one shall hold in contempt or ridicule the religious beliefs of others or excite public hostility against them'.

Freedom of expression

Freedom of expression encompasses the right to hold opinions without interference and to seek, receive and impart information and ideas of all kinds orally, in writing and in any other form and through any media. However, as with all freedoms, it is essential that the right is not unfettered to an extent that an individual may exercise it to the unacceptable disadvantage of other individuals or of the community. In this respect, the African Charter of Human and Peoples' Rights is particularly restrictive in regard to the expression of views. Article 9 provides that every individual shall have the right to receive information, but it goes on to state that an individual 'shall have the right to express and disseminate his opinions *within the law*' (italics added). In effect, this gives a substantially unqualified right to states to make laws restricting the right of individuals to freedom of expression.

Within the other major instruments, the ability of states to interfere with this right is circumscribed. So, for example, under the European Convention the right of the state to interfere with freedom of speech is restricted to the interests of national security, territorial integrity or public safety, or in order to prevent disorder or crime, to protect health or morals, to protect the reputation and rights of others, or to prevent the disclosure of information received in confidence and to maintain the authority and impartiality of the judiciary. A number of applications have been made to the European Commission on Human Rights resulting from the imposition of censorship by states. Most of these come from minority groups who have been prevented from disseminating their ideas for one reason or another. They range from racist organizations through to pacifist organizations. Two major cases have come before the Court, the first arising from the distribution of obscene literature to children, the second concerning the extent to which a state can restrict the publication of information and opinions about matters on which litigation is pending.

The balancing of competing interests is a theme which runs through much of the European case law and this is another area presenting considerable opportunities for comparative study.

The Islamic Declaration of Human Rights provides that every person has the right to express his thoughts and beliefs so long as he remains within the limits prescribed by the Law; Law being derived from Divine Law revealed by Allah. Article 12 of the Declaration goes on to state that no one is entitled to disseminate falsehood or to circulate reports which might outrage public decency, or to indulge in libel.

Right of assembly and association

This has been developing most importantly in recent years in respect of the right to join trade unions. An important corollary to this is the extent to which there is a right not to join trade unions and this is of particular concern in the enforcement or non-enforcement of the concept of the 'closed shop' on which there is an important European case. A number of cases have gone to the European Court of Human Rights concerning the right of association, although in most the claimants have not succeeded in establishing a violation of the rights protected since their claims have usually involved issues of the rights of trade unions themselves, as opposed to the right to join a trade union. The relevant Article of the European Convention, as with other international instruments, is more concerned to protect the right to freedom of association rather than to establish rights for associations.

The relevant Agreements of the International Labour Organization are of much greater significance in this respect [see 182–184 and 506–520]. They include such instruments as the Convention concerning Freedom of Association and Protection of the Right to Organize, the Convention concerning the Application of the Principles of the Right to Organize and to Bargain Collectively and the Convention concerning Protection Facilities to be Afforded to Workers' Representatives in the Undertaking.

This is an area in which there is an obvious overlap of social and civil interests. The right of individual freedom shades into the collectivist interest of social solidarity, as the individual right to join a trade union merges into issues of the closed shop or the rights of unions to be able to negotiate on behalf of their members.

Freedom of movement

The Universal Declaration of Human Rights protects the right of freedom of movement and residence within the borders of a state, including the right of everyone to leave any country, including his own, and to return to his own country. The instrument further provides that everyone has the right to seek and to enjoy asylum from persecution except where this is invoked to avoid prosecution for non-political crimes. In practice, many states restrict internal movement, most frequently for reasons of political and military security, but sometimes for economic and social reasons. It is not uncommon for some totalitarian countries to restrict the right of their nationals to go abroad.

The International Covenant on Civil and Political Rights protects rights of freedom of movement and residence but allows a state to introduce restrictions on the rights in the interests of national security, public order, public health or morals, and for the protection of the rights and freedoms of others. The European Convention, Protocol No. 4, and the American Convention contain similar provisions, and both include a much broader opportunity for the state to restrict freedom of movement on the ground of 'public interest'. This allows states to protect certain areas which are of scientific interest, or which are set aside for conservation or where it is sought to maintain ethnic and cultural traditions. The provision in the African Charter is more restrictive since the individual is given the right to freedom of movement and residence 'provided he abides by the law'.

Although most states are happy to allow freedom of exit subject to the obvious restrictions contained in the European and American Conventions, there is no similar willingness to allow freedom of entry for non-nationals and for refugees. Increasing restriction on immigration is one of the most significant phenomena of recent years.

There are provisions in all three instruments to prohibit the collective deportation and mass expulsion of aliens primarily to prevent racial, ethnic and religious persecution, but beyond these protections there is little to help the individual alien who is ordered to be deported unless he can show that the order in some way amounts to inhuman or degrading treatment or infringes one of the other rights in which he is protected.

The rights of asylum and refuge, although connected with the right to freedom of movement and residence, have an independent history. The granting of asylum to those subject to political persecution has a lengthy history, but is largely a matter of political discretion. Although the right is recognized in the Universal Declaration, it is carefully circumscribed in the American Convention and in the African Charter. In the European Convention, there is nothing more than a procedural protection guaranteeing to the alien the right to be given reasons for his expulsion and the right to have his case reviewed. This is not contained in the original Convention but in Protocol No. 7 to it.

There is a considerable body of literature on the subject and on the wider international problem of refugees [see 557–570].

Right to free elections

The right of the individual to take part in the government of his country, either directly or through freely chosen representatives, is provided for in the Universal Declaration. This also seeks to ensure periodic and genuinely free and representative elections. Similar provisions are contained in the International Covenant, the European Convention, Protocol No. 1, and the American Convention, the latter making much more detailed provision. The right is more circumscribed in the African Charter. The provisions do not provide unqualified rights; aliens, minors and others can be reasonably disenfrachised, and there is no guarantee of proportional representation in the legislature.

Right to property

The Universal Declaration provides that everyone has the right to own property alone and in association with others and that no one shall be arbitrarily deprived of his property. The European and American Conventions both seek to protect the rights of property. This has led to the development of jurisprudence under the ECHR on the circumstances in which states are entitled to expropriate property in the public interest and on the extent to which the state can control the use of property for reasons of fiscal and social policy.

In public international law, the issue is closely tied to whether a state is entitled to expropriate property without paying proper compensation. The expropriation of property belonging to nationals of the expropriating state is not a matter for public international law, but the protection afforded by the European and American Conventions can be relevant and in this respect the judgment of the European Court of Human Rights in the *Lithgow* case is of special importance.

The African Charter protects the right of property but provides that the state may interfere with the right in the interests of public need, or in the general interest of the community. The Islamic Declaration provides that property may not be expropriated except in the public interest and goes on to specify that expropriation must be in the context of fair and adequate compensation.

Right to education

The Universal Declaration provides that everyone has the right to education and that this should be free at the elementary stage. It further provides that technical and professional education should be generally available and that higher education should be equally accessible to all on the basis of merit. In reality, the right to education is more of a social right than a matter of political and civil liberty, and this is reflected in the wording of the Universal Declaration which borders on social engineering in providing that education should be directed, among other things, to the full development of the human personality and to the strengthening of respect for human rights and fundamental freedoms.

Unlike most civil rights, the right to education requires considerable public expenditure if the obligations of the state are to be properly fulfilled. The American Declaration of the Rights and Duties of Man of 1948 contains phrasing which would be a credit to any socialist state. Among other things, Article 12 of the Declaration provides:

> The right to an education includes the right to equality of opportunity in every case, in accordance with natural talents, merit and the desire to utilise the resources that the state or the community is in a position to provide.

The right to education does not figure in the American Convention, nor in the International Covenant on Civil and Political Rights. It is included in the International Convention on Economic, Social and Cultural Rights and in the First Protocol to the European Convention. The emphasis in the European Protocol is very much on the right of the individual not to be denied the right to education whilst at the same time no obligation is laid on the state to provide it, though the Article presupposes that the state will provide some form of education and gives to parents the right to ensure that education and teaching is in conformity with their religious and philosophical convictions.

The African Charter provides a right to education, without specifying any responsibility on the state to provide it. It also ensures that the individual shall have the right freely to take part in the cultural life of the community. Interestingly, it is left to the Universal Islamic Declaration to provide that every person is entitled to receive education in accordance with his natural abilities. Of course, the Universal Islamic Declaration is not a binding treaty.

Right to economic and social provision

The obligation on the state to make social and economic provision for the individual citizen is firmly entrenched in socialist philosophy but, although all Western states make some provision to ensure social security, at least to the elderly and infirm, this is often seen as a matter of grace rather than as a fundamental obligation of indisputable ideological rightness. Attitudes have been changing, and this has been helped by developing international treaty obligations dating back to some of the earlier agreements concluded under the auspices of the International Labour Organization. Article 55 of the United Nations Charter speaks of the promoting 'higher standards of living, full employment, and conditions of economic and social progress and development'. Several of the rights defined in the Universal Declaration on Human Rights are essentially socio-economic. These include the right to social security, the right to work, to free choice of employment, to just and favourable conditions of work and to protection against unemployment. The Declaration also includes the right to equal pay and to just and favourable remuneration, the right to rest and leisure, and to a standard of living adequate for the health and well-being of the individual and his family. Many of these rights are explored in the literature relating to employment rights [see 506–520].

The European Social Charter seeks to protect and develop these and similar rights among the member states of the Council of Europe, on which see D. Harris, *The European Social Charter* [448], but the principal international instrument is the International Covenant on Economic, Social and Cultural Rights. This details the obligation on states to recognize the right of everyone to work and to have the opportunity to gain his own living. Under its provisions, individual states ratifying the treaty undertake to develop programmes of technical and vocational training, to recognize the rights of everyone to fair and just remuneration, to freedom to join trade unions, to social security, to protection for the family, to an adequate standard of living, to the highest technical standard of physical and mental health, to educational development, and so on.

The Treaty of Rome establishing the European Economic Community, although concerned not with the protection of human rights but rather with the establishing of a common economic community between the member states, does have implications for economic and social rights in regard to such matters as freedom of movement of workers and various other enforceable community rights with include among others the right to equal pay. The reader is referred to A. G. Toth's *Legal Protection of Individuals in the European Communities* [460].

Collective Human Rights

Especially in Third World countries, recent thinking has placed increasing significance on the collective rights of peoples. The starting point in the recognition of the rights of peoples is to be found in the United Nations Charter. Under Article 73, states undertake to ensure that the inhabitants of non-self-governing territories shall be ensured due respect for their culture, their political, economic, social and educational advancement, and for their just treatment and protection against abuses. This Article also seeks to develop the right to self-government, to international peace and security, and the promotion of constructive measures of development.

The right to self-determination and political independence has been recognized by successive Resolutions of the General Assembly and is inscribed in Article 1 of the International Covenant on Economic, Social and Cultural Rights. The right goes beyond a right of political self-determination in the narrow sense. Article 1 of the International Covenant on Economic, Social and Cultural Rights seeks to develop the right to enable people, not merely freely to determine their political status, but freely to pursue their economic, social and cultural development. This entails ensuring that peoples are able to dispose of their natural wealth and resources.

As might be expected, it is the African Charter on Human and Peoples' Rights which most substantially develops the philosophy underlying the concept of collective rights of people to self-determination and freedom to dispose of their wealth and natural resources as they choose.

The literature on this subject is considerable. That on genocide is relevant in respect of the most extreme forms of persecution of peoples [see 536–539]. So also is the literature on the treatment of minorities and their protection [551–556]. But the most rapidly developing subjects are undoubtedly the right of self-determination and associated economic rights including sovereignty over natural resources [see 540–550].

4 Human Rights Organizations

Although the origins of humanitarian concern for the rights and freedoms of man owe much to the efforts of many dedicated individuals, ultimately the protection of individuals is very much dependent on the work of international, regional and national organizations, both governmental and non-governmental.

Within the United Nations, the General Assembly has taken a major interest in human and peoples' rights. Mention has already been made of the General Assembly's Universal Declaration of Human Rights and the subsequent International Covenants on Civil and Political Rights and on Economic, Social and Cultural Rights, and also the early establishment of the UN Commission on Human Rights. The documentation of the United Nations in the field of human rights is the most important international source material available to the researcher; the principal sources available are listed in Part II [138–181].

The United Nations is far from being alone among international organizations which protect human rights. The principal governmental international organizations relevant to the protection of human rights fall into two categories. The first are those concerned with particular areas of human activity, such as the International Labour Organization [617] and the International Red Cross [616]. The others which have been particularly important in the development of human rights are the regional organizations under whose auspices the various regional conventions have been developed. Principal among these are the Organization of American States [620], the Council of Europe [611], the Organization of African Unity [619] and the League of Arab States [618], whose main work has been the development of the international human rights instruments discussed above.

Another important regional organization is the European Economic Community [613]. Although principally concerned with the establishment of a common free market economy, the Commission, Council and Parliament of the European Community have proclaimed their respect for fundamental human rights and there has been serious consideration that the European Community should adhere to the European Convention on Human Rights in a corporate capacity. The Court of Justice of the European Community, which is primarily concerned with the interpretation of the treaties and regulations and directives made by the Community, has repeatedly asserted its recognition of fundamental human rights as part of the general principles of law to be followed within the framework of Community law.

Outside of governmental organizations, there are several non-governmental organizations whose concern it is to protect and develop human rights and freedoms. Among the best known of these are bodies such as the International Commission of Jurists [649], Amnesty International [634] and, in ways which are functional rather than political, one cannot ignore the most important work done by bodies such as the World Council of Churches and the very many charities with specific purposes of caring for the sick, needy and undernourished.

In Part III, addresses are provided of the principal organizations which are concerned in the development and protection of human rights politically and legally; these are the bodies whose work and publications are most relevant to researchers and students.

5 The Literature of Human Rights

It will already be clear to the reader that the range of human rights literature of interest to the student and researcher is very varied but, unfortunately, given the nature of the subject and the currency of many of the issues, it is not always readily available and may be subject to considerable delay in publication. This is particularly true in the case of some materials emanating from the major international and non-governmental agencies active in the field, many of which are primarily intended for use within the particular organization rather than by the general public. An attempt to indicate some of the problem areas in this respect is made in Part II.

As far as the broad range of published materials are concerned, those of interest to the human rights researcher may be divided into primary sources, such as treaties, other international instruments, official documentation and case law, which form the basic core for research, and secondary sources such as monographs and periodicals, which comment on the existing state of human rights protection. One must also consider the basic bibliographies, indexes and reference works which provide access to the subject. Outlined in this chapter are some of the basic sources which may be regarded as essential for the student or researcher when he first comes into the field.

Treaties and International Instruments

For serious research, the starting point must be the international treaty protection of human rights, and pre-eminent here are the conventions which have been the principal consideration in the introduction to this volume. They are readily available, both in the various treaty series such as the *United Nations Treaty Series* [3] and *European Treaty Series* [see 9] and in many of the major monographs and journals.

Basic bibliographic details of the main treaty series are provided in Part II [1–10]. It is important to the researcher to be able to access the many international treaties and instruments which provide various specific protections. These again are listed [17–109], with details of the state of ratification of these treaties as at 1 January 1986. The list cannot be totally comprehensive since it is possible for treaties to offer some human rights protection quite incidentally to the main thrust of the agreement. It has also not been possible to list all those International Labour Conventions which offer some degree of protection to those in employment. Rather, an attempt has been made to list those treaties of general international significance whose primary thrust is humanitarian.

As far as the location of treaties is concerned, index sources such as the *Multilateral Treaties: Index and Current Status* produced by Bowman and Harris [11] and the *World Treaty Index* [15] are particularly useful; a list of such indexes is provided in Part II [11–16].

Constitutions

Although this work is strictly concerned with the international legal protection of human rights, the researcher may wish to have regard to the degree of human rights protection which is afforded by the constitutions of particular states. Detailed coverage of national constitutions is not provided, but one or two of the major sources reprinting national constitutions are listed in Part II. Pre-eminent among these printed sources are the multi-volume works produced by Blaustein and Flanz, entitled *Constitutions of the Countries of the World* [110] and Peaslee, *Constitutions of Nations* [112].

Case Law

The third important area of source material, especially for the legal researcher, is the case reporting and written opinions of the various judicial and arbitral bodies, whose function it is to mediate and adjudicate on complaints of human rights violations under the various treaties. As has been pointed out, pre-eminent among these in terms of the development of an international jurisprudence of human rights is the European Court of Human Rights. Since the *Lawless* case back in 1960, the European Commission and Court have considered many disputes, although only a minority of cases have been declared admissible. Although a few cases have been brought before the Inter-American Commission and Court of Human Rights, case law under the American Charter is as yet in its infancy, and no cases have yet been brought under the African Charter which is not yet in force. It is worth noting that other regional bodies not traditionally associated with human rights questions, such as the Court of Justice of the European Communities, have occasionally been called upon to decide cases with human rights aspects, particularly in relation to economic and labour disputes.

At an international level, although action by the International Court of Justice in the area has been limited, there is no doubt that such cases could fall within its competency and, indeed, some of its decisions have dealt with human rights issues. In the area of international human rights violations, much useful work is done by the various subsidiary bodies of the United Nations and many of their reports and declarations, although not strictly falling into the area of case law, have served to bring action to remedy violations.

Various specialist series exist to provide coverage of human rights cases. As far as cases on the European Convention are concerned, the Council of Europe produces a range of documentation, ranging from mimeographed copies of new decisions and judgments [127, 130 and 131] which are available on request, to summaries of recent Commission decisions [129] and, in association with the West German publisher Carl Heymanns, full reports of cases which reach the European Court, along with details of the pleadings and arguments employed [125 and 126]. Significant cases are also reprinted in the *Yearbook of the European Convention on Human Rights* [132]. Full details of all these series are provided in Part II. However, arguably the most useful set is a commercially produced series under the title *European Human Rights Reports* [137], which covers all significant European cases as well as reprinting other relevant human rights documentation. This series provides fairly speedy coverage of new decisions.

As noted above, case law under the American Convention is as yet in its infancy. Decisions may be available on request from the Inter-American Commission in mimeographed form. However, summaries of Inter-American case law will also be found in *European Human Rights Reports* [137] and the *Human Rights Law Journal* [265].

Whilst mentioning periodicals, it is worth noting that many of those listed in Part II provide useful summaries of new case law, although they do not seek to provide full coverage of cases. Summaries of decisions in the *Human Rights Law Journal* [265] and *European Law Review* [257] are particularly useful in this respect. Several index series provide access to cases brought before the various international and regional human rights bodies. The *European Law Digest* [256] provides a useful service, as well as summarizing decisions of national courts on the topic, and the Council of Europe has produced its own indexes of past decisions, *e.g.* [129]. Other tools such as *Current Law* [236] may also be useful.

Official Documentation

Treaties and case law provide perhaps the primary source materials for the human rights researcher who is interested in the international legal protection of human rights. However, he must also be aware at the outset of the wide range of official documentation, some of which may be regarded as source material and some of which serves to comment on human rights activities, which emanates from international and regional organizations active in the field. Much of this material may not be readily accessible to the general student, although some bodies, particularly the Council of Europe, are very helpful in making literature available.

An attempt to list some of the most important series, both international and regional, is made in Part II [138–231]. Here are merely indicated a few of the titles which may be particularly useful to the researcher coming newly to the subject.

The United Nations and its subsidiary bodies have produced a vast amount of documentation relating to human rights matters but, unfortunately, this is not always easy to locate through the various printed indexes which are available. Perhaps the most useful introductory work is the volume entitled *United Nations Action in the Field of Human Rights* [173]. This presents a detailed study of United Nations involvement in the area between its creation and the end of 1982. Many UN documents are summarized and full references are provided for General Assembly resolutions and other documentation. Two other UN series are worthy of note as introductory works. The United Nations *Yearbook* [169] provides a broad overview of developments in all areas including human rights, alongside full references to original documentation. Unfortunately the series is fairly slow to appear. Another series which is even slower in appearance, the United Nations *Yearbook on Human Rights* [170], again provides useful summaries of activity and references to full documentation.

These three summaries provide perhaps the best introduction to United Nations activity and should satisfy the needs of many students. It must be emphasized that for the general reader, United Nations documentation is not easy to follow, and one may soon get lost in the mass of paper which emanates from its many committees. There are several indexes to UN publications [see 138–149], but many working documents which are primarily designed for internal use may neither be easy to trace nor to obtain in practice. A current listing of UN documents is available in the *UNDOC: Current index* [146] which has appeared since 1979. Earlier publications were covered in the *United Nations Documents Index* which covered the period 1950–73 [143] and the *UNDEX* series [145] which covered the 1970s. A further useful bibliography on the work of the United Nations, listing many important secondary sources compiled by Hufner and Naumann [299], should also be noted. Documents produced by the League of Nations in the inter-war period may be traced through an index produced by Aufricht [138].

Various other international bodies have produced a mass of useful documentation. Although the International Labour Organization is primarily concerned with employment matters, these are often associated with the rights of individuals, and the Organization has produced a large amount of pertinent conventions and documentation over the years. Only the most significant agreements concluded under the auspices of the Organization are listed in the treaty chapter, but the basic conventions from 1919–81 are collected together in one volume [6]. Information on more recent legislative activity is collected in the thrice-yearly *Official Bulletin* [189], and relevant items may also be noted in the monthly *International Labour Review* [187] or *Social and Labour Bulletin* which summarize the Organization's activities. Several indexes to ILO documentation are available [see 182–185].

Although the main UNESCO activity lies outside the area of human rights, it has produced some relevant documentation, especially in the educational field. New UNESCO activities in the area are summarized in the *UNESCO Chronicle* [180] and *UNESCO Courier* [181]. Useful detailed indexes to UNESCO documentation are available [175-177].

The International Committee of the Red Cross is not directly linked to the United Nations but is worthy of mention here as a major international organization concerned with the protection of human rights in the sphere of humanitarian law. Useful summaries of Red Cross activities are listed in Part II, and the reader is particularly referred to the bi-monthly *International Review of the Red Cross* [195] and the *International Red Cross Handbook* [197].

Regional organizations are of major importance when one examines the development of human rights protection. The Council of Europe has been the most active and an extensive list of materials emanating from that Organization is provided in Part II [198-220]. One or two of the reports and treaty series produced by the Council are noted above but, as far as general surveys of activity are concerned, perhaps the most useful publication is the *Yearbook of the European Convention on Human Rights* [213] which summarizes developments each year, with details of recent cases and other documentary references. It is somewhat quicker to appear than some of the other yearbooks, but for up-to-date information on human rights matters the reader is referred to series such as *Activities of the Council of Europe in the Field of Human Rights* [202] and the general *Information Bulletin on Legislative Activities* [207]. The Council of Europe has also produced single-volume texts collecting the major human rights conventions [217] and summarizing its activity in the field [220]. Reference to Council of Europe publications may be obtained through their annual sales catalogue, and occasional mimeographed listings of 'Publications in the field of human rights' [200 and 201]. A useful bibliography on Council of Europe activity detailing much valuable secondary material on the European Convention and its practice was published back in 1978 [198] but now needs updating.

Although the Inter-American Commission on Human Rights has been in existence for twenty years, it has been far less active than its European counterpart and has produced considerably less documentation. The most useful sources are listed in Part II [221-231]. Noteworthy is the *Inter-American Yearbook on Human Rights* [225] although this is extremely slow to appear. Summaries of human rights activity are included in the OAS *Legal Newsletter* [226]. Annual reports of Commission activity are also prepared [*e.g.* 223], although these may not be easy to obtain. The reader should also note a few useful single-volume summaries of IACHR activity. *The Handbook of Existing Rules Pertaining to Human Rights in the Inter-American System* [228] reprints most OAS documents and regulations in the area, and a volume entitled *Ten Years of Activities* gives a useful survey of IACHR activity from 1971-81 [231]. Bibliographic details of OAS publications are provided in a couple of Spanish series [221-222] and an English catalogue is available.

If documentation on the American Convention is difficult to obtain, then the situation with regard to Africa and the Islamic world is extremely dismal. The addresses of the Organization of African Unity [619] and League of Arab States [618] are listed in Part III, and the interested reader may be able to obtain relevant material by direct approach to these groups. Summaries of their activities may also be obtainable in some of the general texts and periodicals which are listed in Part II [see particularly 423].

For information on documentation from the major non-governmental organizations active in the field, the reader is referred to the individual entries in Part III. In many cases their publications and documentation may be extremely valuable. Often, unfortunately, it is extremely elusive. Only the more important non-governmental organizations are listed in Part III, but fuller listings are available in the valuable guides produced by Human Rights Internet [604–606].

Secondary Sources

Although the original materials are key sources for the human rights researcher, they will not satisfy all information needs and the student may indeed be deterred by the technicality of much of the original documentation. Textbooks and monographs commenting on the development of human rights law serve as essential introductory materials. Even the advanced researcher may value their discussion and interpretations of particular human rights problems. Such commentaries may be found in the mass of periodical and monograph literature which is available in the field, and an attempt has been made to list some of the most important materials in Part II.

Periodicals

In such a rapidly developing area, it is not surprising that periodical literature is of major importance, enabling the reader to keep up to date with the latest developments in the field. In this survey, only an overview of the sources is provided. It is impossible to give individual references to the thousands of articles written on the topic. Such work has been attempted in more detailed bibliographies and indexes, notably that by Friedman and Sherman [316] and others which are listed in Part II. A few titles concerning themselves specifically with human rights call for special comment. The leading European English language serial is the *Human Rights Law Journal* [265] published under the auspices of the International Institute of Human Rights. This journal carries a few articles in each issue, but is mainly concerned to provide full commentary on contemporary developments and cases in the field. It now incorporates the *Human Rights Review* [267] published between 1976 and 1981. Two or three other British- and European-based series are worthy of mention. The *European Law Review* [257], which appears six times a year, provides a full commentary on recent decisions of the European Commission and Court of Human Rights. Articles on human rights also appear from time to time in other serials such as the *British Year Book of International Law* [250] and the *International and Comparative Law Quarterly* [272]. The *Review* [273] produced by the

International Commission of Jurists also contains some useful material.

American journals with titles relating to human rights often have a bias towards civil rights coverage, rather than the international protection of human rights. Such is the case, for example, with the *Columbia Human Rights Law Review* [255]. One or two series such as the *Human Rights Quarterly* [266] are of value, as is the *American Journal of International Law* [247] which has included a number of seminal articles on the subject. Perhaps the most useful US-based serial is the *Human Rights Internet Reporter* [263], which provides valuable journalistic coverage of new developments in all parts of the world. Similar digests of new events, although not especially related to human rights matters, are provided by *Facts on File* [258] and in Britain by *Keesings Contemporary Archives* [277]. Human rights documents may be reprinted in one or two serials, including most usefully *International Legal Materials* [275] which includes a selection of treaty material as well as other UN documentation.

As far as bibliographies and index sources relating to periodicals are concerned, there are several guides which are of value to the researcher. Full bibliographic details of most serial titles can be found in *Ulrich's International Periodicals Directory* [235] and the associated listing of irregular serials [232]. In tracing journal articles in the field of human rights, the lawyer is well served by a couple of major sources. The *Index to Legal Periodicals*, produced by the Wilson company [240], and the *Index to Foreign Legal Periodicals* [239], published by the Institute of Advanced Legal Studies and the American Association of Law Libraries, between them cover the majority of English and foreign language law journals. *Public International Law: A current bibliography of articles* produced by the Max Planck Institute [243] is also of value. As noted above, the major human rights bibliography produced by Friedman and Sherman [316] is of great utility in tracing journal articles, as are other bibliographic monographs. Human rights articles may also be traced by recourse to more general sources listing materials in newspapers and general serials, such as the *British Humanities Index* and the useful *Public Affairs Information Service Bulletin* [306].

Bibliographies

Mention of bibliographic sources relating to periodicals leads one on to consider those sources which may be of value in tracing the many monographs which have appeared on the subject of human rights. In the past few years a number of bibliographies have been produced as an aid to the researcher coming into the field. The fact that such guides are a fairly recent phenomenon may be illustrated by the fact that the classic bibliographic guide by Besterman [290] lists no bibliographies specifically on human rights, although it notes several in the general area of international law. However, the supplement to Besterman, covering the period 1964–74, compiled by Toomey [312], lists half a dozen relevant bibliographies. It must, however, be remembered that in such a rapidly developing field, bibliographies quickly become outdated, whilst few are of any value in tracing documentation.

Several general bibliographic guides may be of use when gathering materials on the subject. As far as law-based guides are concerned, the 4-volume bibliography *Law Books 1876–1981*, produced by Bowker [302], lists a large number of human rights texts indexed under the general heading of civil rights. The information given there is updated by *Law Information* [304] from the same publisher which provides an annual listing of new texts by author and subject. The annual *Bibliographic Guide to Law* [291] published by Hall provides a similar listing of new material.

General national bibliographies and catalogues such as the *British National Bibliography* and *Library of Congress Catalog* should not be forgotten when searching for particular human rights titles. Other library catalogues may also be useful. The Harvard Law School Library *Annual Legal Bibliography* [297] provided a comprehensive listing of new books and journal articles coming into that library until the set ceased in 1981. Information contained in the series has to some extent been updated by a new cumulation although at present this does not index journals. Other guides to library holdings are mentioned at the end of Part II [608–610].

Human rights questions are of interest to many people other than lawyers. The *Public Affairs Information Service Bulletin* [306] is a valuable tool indexing many legal, political and general interest serials and monographs. One or two other series more concerned with political aspects of human rights questions should also be mentioned. The *International Bibliography of Political Science* [301] produced each year as part of the *International Bibliography of the Social Sciences* lists a range of new journal and monograph articles in the field, while short abstracts of significant items are provided in the annual volume of *International Political Science Abstracts*. Finally, as far as ongoing bibliographic sources are concerned, mention should be made of the *Checklist of Human Rights Documents* [313] produced by the Tarlton Law Library of the University of Texas. This series provided access to a mass of new documentation in the field but ceased publication in 1980, leaving a vacuum which is only partly filled by the invaluable *Human Rights Internet Reporter* [263]. Several individual bibliographies have been produced in the past few years, although it must be remembered that these soon become outdated. Books on human rights are listed in one or two general legal bibliographies, such as the useful *Lawyers' Law Books* [307] now in its second edition. Two general bibliographies on international law, one compiled by Delupis in 1975 [315] and one produced by Merrills in 1978 [332], concentrating on journal articles written in the last twenty years, may throw up some useful introductory material. That by Delupis, in particular, lists a large number of items relating to human rights, although unfortunately it is now a little outdated.

Other more specialized bibliographies are listed in Part II, but one or two are worthy of special note. Perhaps the most important source is a recently published bibliography, *Human Rights: an international and comparative law bibliography*, compiled by Friedman and Sherman [316] which lists over 4,000 monographs and journal articles in several languages relating to all aspects of human rights. It also includes a valuable listing of more general sources. Unfortunately, the bibliography is not annotated. *Human Rights: A topical bibliography* [314] compiled by the Columbia University Center for the Study of Human Rights, listing 2,500 items, offers a similar service. A series of valuable articles by Diana Vincent-Daviss which appeared in the *New York University Journal of International Law and Politics* [345-347] in 1981 and 1982 provides access to a large range of human rights materials, ranging from original documentation to books and serials. Another broad overview of the literature was provided in a valuable article by Reynolds which appeared in the *Law Library Journal* in 1978 [337]. This article was particularly valuable for its overview of official documentation. Finally, the reader should not forget the useful bibliographies which are often appended to general texts. In the bibliography chapter, only one is listed, that included in Vasak's useful survey [344], but many others are of value.

As far as regional coverage of the subject is concerned, the researcher is tolerably well served by existing bibliographies. Some of the general titles listed above, notably Friedman and Sherman [316], provide an extensive listing of regional materials. For Europe, the *Bibliography Relating to the European Convention on Human Rights* produced by the Council of Europe back in 1978 stands out [198]. Unfortunately this title is badly in need of revision. For the Americas, the Library of Congress guide to *Human Rights in Latin America* [331] is noteworthy, and a number of short articles on regional human rights protection by Richard Greenfield which appeared in *Human Rights Quarterly* [319-322] should also be mentioned.

A number of specialized bibliographies on particular aspects of human rights issues have appeared, including those of ILO human rights activities [327 and 328], and surveys of international criminal law and humanitarian law. Again, individual titles are listed in Part II.

Monographs

In Part II some 237 monographs are listed, divided into classifications to help the reader. It is not easy to comment on more than a small number at this point but, bearing in mind the value of an up-to-date text, the reader seeking an introduction to the subject is recommended to read the recently published *The Lawful Rights of Mankind* by P. Sieghart [386]. At a more technical level, that same author's *The International Law of Human Rights* [385] is a valuable work. Useful source books for the student include Brownlie's *Basic Documents on Human Rights* [371] and Drzemczewski's *Cases and Materials on Human Rights* [373], and a very useful selection of extracted texts is contained in *International Protection of Human Rights* by Sohn and Buergenthal [387].

The International Dimensions of Human Rights edited by K. Vasak [423] is a most important and valuable collection of essays. It is one of the few works to contain essays on the less well-covered areas of the subject including the protection of human rights in Africa and Islam.

The best elementary introduction to the European Convention is by Beddard

[441]. Most of the main books on the subject are out of date because of the rapidly developing case law, but the best accounts are those by Castberg [442], Fawcett [446] and Jacobs [450]. More up to date is the textbook by Van Dijk and Van Hoof [461] available in a revised English translation.

The major work on the Inter-American system is undoubtedly Buergenthal and Norris's *Human Rights: The Inter-American System* in three volumes [464]. Together with D. Shelton, these same authors produced *Protecting Human Rights in the Americas* [465] in 1982 which is the nearest thing to an up-to-date textbook on the subject.

Reference Works

In Part 2 are listed some of the major reference works, directories and dictionaries which may be of value to the researcher. These include language glossaries [591–597] and directories of human rights organizations [601–606]. As far as directories are concerned, by far the most valuable are those produced by Human Rights Internet [604–606] which list national and international organizations working in the field of human rights in all areas of the world.

Non-governmental Organizations

Aside from the international law of human rights is the vitally important issue of the level of state regard for human rights and freedoms. Here the documentation of the United Nations is the principal repository of information, and reference has been made to this. But several other organizations are assiduous in their documentation of human rights developments and violations. Principal among these are the International Commission of Jurists [649] and Amnesty International [634]. The key groups are listed in Part III, but it needs to be remembered that there are an enormous number of bodies around the world interested in aspects of human rights. The fullest listing is contained in the Human Rights Internet series [604–606]; many of these produce documentation and reports. In the case of the more important groups listed in Part III, attention is drawn to those which produce useful documentation.

Library Collections

It is important for the human rights student or researcher to be able to gain access to the various different types of material surveyed in this volume. Unfortunately, this may not always be easy. Basic human rights literature may be found in all types of library, from the larger public libraries through university and college collections to the major national repositories. In many cases, requests for secondary materials not available in the reader's own library may be met from another collection through an inter-library loans scheme. Such a scheme may also help in requests for the more important primary materials and original documentation but, although the major national and university collections will generally hold at least some of the original source materials listed in Part II, they are not always willing to make these available on loan to the outside reader. In such cases he will be forced to visit other libraries if he is to continue his research.

A few guides to library collections are listed, including a valuable one by Garling on London libraries, at the end of Part II [608–610]. It is also worth noting the guide to printed library catalogues by Nelson [305]. Printed library catalogues for significant law and politics collections, such as the Institute of Advanced Legal Studies and the London School of Economics' *London Bibliography of the Social Sciences*, may indicate whether or not a particular volume is held by another library before a visit is made. Increasingly with the development of online library catalogues, remote searches of another library's holdings become more feasible. It should, however, be stressed that conventional library catalogues may not list holdings of official publications so that such searches should be undertaken with care. Indeed, as noted elsewhere, although the major academic and national collections will hold many of the basic source materials listed in Part II, they are by no means all readily available. This is particularly true in the case of publications from the United Nations, which are often intended purely for internal use. If any problems are encountered in tracing such material, it will be necessary to call on the assistance of specialist library staff.

Classification Schemes

Although official documentation creates its own difficulties, most categories of human rights material can be traced through conventional library catalogues. There are several different classification schemes in general use in libraries to aid the location of materials. Most public library collections make use of the Dewey Decimal system, while the Library of Congress scheme is often employed by universities. UDC or Universal Decimal Classification may also be encountered.

The index to the Dewey system does not recognize the existence of human rights, rather referring the researcher to the related term of civil rights. However, within the actual classification schedule, the term human rights is used on at least one occasion. There are three basic areas where the subject is encountered: these being within the schedules for political science, and within municipal law and international law. Civil rights in their political aspect are generally allocated class numbers between 323.4 and 323.6 in the section of the schedule dealing with the relation of the state to individuals. Within this broad area, the number 323.4 is assigned to civil rights, 323.5 to political rights and 323.6 to citizenship and related topics, each number being further subdivided into individual rights and freedoms. Within law, the number 342.085 is assigned to individual rights in municipal law, 342.083 being assigned to citizenship and nationality. In the field of international law, the area of 341.48 is concerned with jurisdiction over persons, 341.481 covers basic human rights and 341.482 nationality and citizenship.

Within the UDC system of classification, rather more provision is made for the subject of civil and political rights. The area of 342.7 is assigned to rights, liberties, freedoms and guarantees secured to citizens and societies. Within this field, further subdivisions deal with particular rights. Thus, for example, 342.724 is assigned to racial equality and 342.734 is assigned to the right to work. A feature of the UDC system is that its rather more complex notation allows a greater degree of specificity than can be achieved by the Dewey Decimal classification. In particular, it should be noted that the schedule (100) applied to any of the subject groupings within the field 342.7 applies particularly to the human rights aspect of the subject.

Material on human rights is rather scattered within the loosely organized Library of Congress classification scheme, and within law the problems of the researcher are exacerbated by the fact that the complete schedules have not yet appeared. As a result, many libraries have adopted their own classification scheme for law, or adapted other published schedules, such as that by Moys, to cover the subject. Particular aspects of the topic of human rights are dealt with in four different areas of the Library of Congress schedules. It receives some limited coverage within classes B and H. Class B deals with philosophy and religion and allocates a number to civil rights and theology at BT738.15. Within the broad field of class H, dealing with economic affairs, various numbers are allocated to aspects of the subject. Thus, for example, the right to work and the right to partake in union membership are dealt with at HD4903 and HD6488. However, the main numbers which deal with human rights topics are to be found in class J which deals with politics and class K which deals with law. Civil rights and liberties in their political aspects are dealt with between class numbers JC571 and JC609 in the schedules.

Within the general and comparative law schedule, class K, civil and political rights and topics relating to the protection of human rights are dealt with between K3236 and K3268. General human rights protection is covered first and this is followed by numbers allocated to particular rights. Other schedules dealing with the laws of a particular country or area also allocate numbers to human rights. Thus in class KD dealing with English law, the section following KD4080 deals with civil and political rights in the country. As mentioned above, some law libraries employ the Moys classification scheme for law in preference to the incomplete Library of Congress schedules. This allocates the numbers KM200–209 to human rights law and KC200–208 to international human rights law.

PART II

Sources of information

6 Treaties and Other International Instruments

Human rights protection in international law is almost wholly the result of provisions made in treaties and other international instruments. The references in this chapter individually list those international and regional treaties which are of current significance in the protection of human rights [17–85] and also various UN Resolutions and other Declarations which are of importance [86–109]. Also listed are the most important international collections of treaties and other materials [1–10] and the more useful collections of indexes [11–16].

Treaty Series

International

1 Parry, C. (ed.). *Consolidated Treaty Series*. Dobbs Ferry, New York: Oceana, 1969–81. 231 vols, plus indexes.
Covers treaties concluded between 1648 and 1919, although few of these are of more than historical interest to human rights researchers.

2 *League of Nations. Treaty series. Publication of treaties and international engagements registered with the Secretariat of the League of Nations*. Geneva: League of Nations, 1920–46. 205 vols.
Covers inter-war period.

3 *United Nations. Treaty series. Treaties and international agreements registered or filed and recorded with the Secretariat of the United Nations*. New York: United Nations, 1946–. Over 1,000 vols published by 1985.
Although this is the basic source for post-war treaties, there is a considerable time lag in publication and it may be ten years before a treaty is published in this series.

For the individual treaties listed below [17–85], reference is generally provided to one of the above series. However, in the case of more recent agreements, or those few others which are not included in these main series, it is necessary to consult alternative sources. Many agreements are included in official series such as the *British and Foreign State Papers*, the Treaty Series included in the United Kingdom Command Papers or the *United States Treaty Series*. Command Papers, published by HMSO, cover a wide range of issues and have appeared in several numerical sequences. Those published between 1900 and 1918 bore the prefix 'Cd', between 1919 and 1956 'Cmd' and those published from 1956 have appeared under the prefix 'Cmnd'. Details of Command Papers may be obtained from the annual HMSO publications catalogue.

4 *British and Foreign State Papers 1373–1968*. London: HMSO, 1832–1977. 170 vols.
This series has now ceased but is worthy of note as some of the earlier instruments are not readily available elsewhere.

5 *US Treaties and Other International Agreements*. Washington: US Dept. of State, 1950–. Annual.
Replaces Bevans, C. I. *Treaties and Other International Acts of the USA 1776–1949*. Washington: US Dept. of State, 1968. 12 vols.

It is often possible to trace the text of recent instruments in commercially produced series such as *International Legal Materials* [275], the *American Journal of International Law* [247] or the *European Human Rights Reports* [137]. Various collections of documents by writers such as Brownlie, listed in the monograph chapter [371], provide convenient access to the major instruments.

Several more specialized collections should also be noted:

6 International Labour Office. *International Labour Conventions and Recommendations 1919–1981*. Geneva: ILO, 1981. 1167 pp. plus supplements to 1985.
Many ILO Conventions have human rights implications. Although only a few of the more important ones are listed here, full texts are available in this volume which is periodically updated by supplements. The latest Conventions can be traced through the ILO *Official Bulletin* [189].

7 For UN Resolutions, see **Djonovich, D. J.** (ed.). *United Nations Resolutions. Series I. Resolutions Adopted by the General Assembly*. Dobbs Ferry, New York: Oceana, 1973–. 21 vols so far published covering the period 1946–83.
UN Resolutions are also printed in the *United Nations Yearbook* [169] and the Council of Europe, *Human Rights Information Sheets* [206].

8 United Nations Secretariat. *International Human Rights Instruments of the United Nations 1948–1982*. Pleasantville, New York: UNIFO, 1983. 190 pp.

This is a very useful collection of the more relevant and important UN instruments. See also [171] in the chapter on international documentation, and [431].

Europe

9 Council of Europe. *European Conventions and Agreements.* Strasbourg: Council of Europe, 1971–83. 4 vols, plus index to Vols. 1 and 2.
Provides the text of Conventions up to No. 108 of 1982. By the end of 1985, 121 agreements had been concluded. Conventions are available individually from the Council of Europe in the *European Treaty Series*, and it also publishes a series of explanatory reports outlining the contents of individual agreements.

10 Council of Europe. *Collection of Texts on the European Convention on Human Rights.* Strasbourg: Council of Europe, 1983.
Collections of various materials including texts of the European Convention on Human Rights, its protocols, and rules of procedure of the Court and Commission.

Treaty Indexes

General

11 Bowman, M. J. and **Harris, D. J.** *Multilateral Treaties: Index and current status.* London: Butterworths, 1984. 516 pp. With 3rd cumulative supplement, 1986. 101 pp.
Details the major treaties of the 20th century, providing dates, parties and sources. Includes regional conventions. Kept up to date by supplements. A valuable source of information as to which states have ratified treaties and thereby become bound by them.

12 Kavass, I. I. and **Sprudzs, A.** *A Guide to the United States Treaties in Force. Part 2: Multilateral Treaties and Other Agreements.* Buffalo, New York: Hein, 1984. 346 pp.
Lists treaties to which the USA is a party with information on dates, other parties, etc. *Treaties in Force*, published annually by the US Dept. of State, is also helpful.

13 Millar, T. B. and **Ward, R.** (eds.). *Current International Treaties.* London: Croom Helm, 1984. 558 pp.
Provides text of Universal Declaration and the two major UN covenants. Lists the other main instruments in the field, but without text.

14 Parry, C. and **Hopkins, C.** *An Index of British Treaties 1101–1968.* London: HMSO, 1970. 3 vols.
Details British treaties both bilateral and multilateral up to 1968 and provides access through references to a variety of series. Somewhat outdated as regards human rights instruments.

15 Rohn, P. H. *World Treaty Index*. 2nd ed. Santa Barbara, California/Oxford: ABC-Clio Information Services, 1983–4. 5 vols.
Fullest listing of treaties of the 20th century which are deposited with the UN. Provides brief details of treaty and location of text in *UN Treaty Series*.

Europe
16 Council of Europe. *Chart Showing Signatures and Ratifications of Council of Europe Conventions and Agreements*. Strasbourg: Council of Europe. Updated annually. Current chart available on application.

Other commercially produced index sources are generally too dated to be of much interest to the human rights researcher.

Treaties and Conventions in the Field of Human Rights

International
17 *International Agreement for the Suppression of the White Slave Traffic*. 1904. Signed Paris 18 May 1904 and entered into froce 18 July 1905. 72 parties. Sources: 1 LNTS 83, Cd 2689.
Parties agree to take measures to suppress the traffic in prostitution. See also [25].

18 *International Convention for the Suppression of the White Slave Traffic*. 1910 with 1949 Protocol. Signed Paris 4 May 1910 and entered into force 15 September 1911. 71 parties. Sources: Cd 6326, 103 BFSP 244. 1949 Protocol: 30 UNTS 23.
Parties undertake to make international trafficking in prostitution an offence under their law.

19 *Constitution of the International Labour Organization*. 1919. Signed Versailles 28 June 1919 and entered into force 10 January 1920. 151 parties. Sources: Cmd 7452, USTS 874, 31 AJIL Supplement 67.
The organization was established in the wake of the Treaty of Versailles to promote the economic and social well-being of workers. Many of its Conventions concern themselves with the rights of workers, but only a few of them, specifically concerned with trade union rights, are included here. Reference to the full series of agreements is readily available from ILO sources or via treaty guides such as Bowman and Harris [11].

20 *Convention and Statute on Freedom of Transit*. 1921. Signed Barcelona 20 April 1921 and entered into force 31 October 1922. 42 parties. Sources: 7 LNTS 11, Cmd 1992.
Parties agree to facilitate the passage of all persons through their territories in time of peace regardless of their nationality or destinations.

21 *International Convention on the Suppression of Traffic in Women and Children*. 1921 with 1947 Protocol. Signed Geneva 30 September 1921 and entered into force 28 June 1922. 73 parties. Sources: 9 LNTS 416, Cmd 1986. 1947 Protocol: 53 UNTS 13.

Extends provisions of 1910 Convention on trafficking in prostitution. 1947 Protocol widened access to Convention.

22 *Right of Association (Agriculture) Convention.* 1921. Signed Geneva 12 November 1921 and entered into force 11 May 1923. 110 parties. Sources: 38 UNTS 153, Cmd 1612.

Gives agricultural workers the same rights to combine as those enjoyed by industrial workers.

23 *Slavery Convention.* 1926 with 1953 Protocol. Signed Geneva 25 September 1926 and entered into force 9 March 1927. Amended by Protocol of 7 December 1953. 98 parties, 82 with Protocol. Sources: 60 LNTS 253, Cmd 2910. 1953 Protocol: 182 UNTS 51.

The parties to the original Convention agree on a definition of slavery and to abolish or prevent it in their territories. The 1953 Protocol makes the UN the depository for the Convention and opens it to all states. See also [41].

24 *Forced Labour Convention.* 1930. Signed Geneva 28 June 1930 and entered into force 1 May 1932. 134 parties. Source: 39 UNTS 55.

Parties undertake to suppress forced labour.

25 *International Convention for the Suppression of Traffic in Women of Full Age.* 1933. Signed Geneva 11 October 1933 and entered into force 24 August 1934. 45 parties. Source: 150 LNTS 31.

Extends the scope of earlier white slave agreements. See [17].

26 *United Nations Charter.* 1945. Signed San Francisco 26 June 1945 and entered into force 24 October 1945. 159 parties. Sources: 1 UNTS xvi, Cmd 7015.

Established the United Nations and set out its aims and functions.

27 *Freedom of Association and Protection of the Right to Organize Convention.* 1948. Signed Geneva 9 July 1948 and entered into force 4 July 1950. 97 parties. Sources: 68 UNTS 17, Cmd 7638.

Provides for basic trade union rights.

28 *Convention on the Prevention and Punishment of the Crime of Genocide.* 1948. Signed New York 9 December 1948 and entered into force 12 January 1951. 96 parties. Sources: 78 UNTS 277, Cmd 4421.

Definition of genocide and provides for its international punishment.

29 *Convention on the Right to Organize and to Bargain Collectively.* 1949. Signed Geneva

1 July 1949 and entered into force 18 July 1951. 113 parties. Sources: 96 UNTS 257, Cmd 7852.
Provides for basic trade union rights.

30 *Convention for the Amelioration of the Condition of the Wounded and Sick in Armed Forces in the Field.* 1949. Signed Geneva 12 August 1949 and entered into force 21 October 1950. 162 parties. Sources: 75 UNTS 31, Cmd 550.
Replaces 1929 Geneva Convention of the same title.

31 *Convention for the Amelioration of the Condition of Wounded, Sick and Shipwrecked Members of the Armed Forces at Sea.* 1949. Signatories and sources as [30].
Replaces 1907 Hague Convention on the same subject.

32 *Convention for the Treatment of Prisoners of War.* 1949. Signatories and sources as [30].
Replaces 1929 Geneva Convention.

33 *Convention on the Protection of Civilian Persons in Time of War.* 1949. Signatories and sources as [30].

Collectively, these Conventions [30–33] are known as the Red Cross Conventions. See also [57 and 58].

34 *Convention for the Suppression of Traffic in Persons and of the Exploitation of the Prostitution of Others.* 1950 with Final Protocol. Signed New York 21 March 1950 and entered into force 25 July 1951. 58 parties. Sources: 96 UNTS 271, 157 BFSP 482. Final Protocol: 96 UNTS 316.
Consolidates and extends earlier treaties on prostitution. Protocol allows for stricter legislation on the subject.

35 *Equal Remuneration Convention.* 1951. Signed Geneva 29 June 1951 and entered into force 23 May 1953. 107 parties. Sources: 165 UNTS 303, Cmd 5039.
Supports equal pay for both sexes for work of equal value.

36 *Convention Relating to the Status of Refugees.* 1951. Signed Geneva 28 July 1951 and entered into force 22 April 1954. 96 parties. Sources: 189 UNTS 137, Cmd 9171.
Defines refugees and provides for their protection. See also [54]:

37 *Maternity Protection Convention.* 1952. Signed Geneva 28 June 1952 and entered into force 7 September 1955. 24 parties. Sources: 214 UNTS 321, Cmd 8825.
Provides for maternity leave for women.

38 *Convention on the Political Rights of Women.* 1953. Signed New York 31 March

1953 and entered into force 7 July 1954. 91 parties. Sources: 193 UNTS 135, Cmnd 3449.

Political rights for women.

39 *Convention on the International Right of Correction.* 1953. Signed New York 31 March 1953 and entered into force 24 August 1962. 11 parties. Source: 435 UNTS 191.

Affirms the right to correct false information by mass communication media.

40 *Convention Relating to the Status of Stateless Persons.* 1954. Signed New York 28 September 1954 and entered into force 6 June 1960. 34 parties. Source: 360 UNTS 117.

Provides for rights and duties of stateless persons and their host state.

41 *Supplementary Convention on the Abolition of Slavery, the Slave Trade and Institutions and Practices Similar to Slavery.* 1956. Signed Geneva 7 September 1956 and entered into force 30 April 1957. 101 parties. Sources: 266 UNTS 3, Cmnd 257.

Supplements the 1926 Convention [23].

42 *Convention on the Nationality of Married Women.* 1957. Signed New York 20 February 1957 and entered into force 11 August 1958. 55 parties. Sources: 309 UNTS 65, Cmnd 601.

Creates nationality rights for married women.

43 *Abolition of Forced Labour Convention.* 1957. Signed Geneva 25 June 1957 and entered into force 17 January 1959. 108 parties. Sources: 320 UNTS 291, Cmnd 328.

Parties agree not to make use of compulsory labour.

44 *Discrimination (Employment and Occupation) Convention.* 1958. Signed Geneva 25 June 1958 and entered into force 15 June 1960. 107 parties. Sources: 362 UNTS 31, Cmnd 593.

Provides for the elimination of discrimination in employment on grounds of race and sex.

45 *Convention Against Discrimination in Education.* 1960 with 1962 Protocol. Signed Paris 14 December 1960 and entered into force 22 May 1962. (Protocol in force 1968.) 77 parties, 29 to Protocol. Sources: 429 UNTS 93, Cmnd 1760. 1962 Protocol: 651 UNTS 362.

Provides for equality of opportunity in education. 1962 Protocol establishes a Good Offices Commission to seek settlement of disputes between parties to the Convention.

46 *Convention on the Reduction of Statelessness.* 1961. Signed New York 30 August 1961 and entered into force 13 December 1975. 14 parties. Sources: 989 UNTS 175, Cmnd 6364.
Attempts to reduce statelessness by regulating nationality rights.

47 *Equality of Treatment (Social Security) Convention.* 1962. Signed Geneva 28 June 1962 and entered into force 25 April 1964. 35 parties. Sources: 494 UNTS 271, Cmnd 1833.
Provides for equality of treatment in social security matters for nationals and non-nationals.

48 *Convention on Consent to Marriage, Minimum Age for Marriage and Regulation of Marriages.* 1962. Signed New York 10 December 1962 and entered into force 9 December 1964. 34 parties. Sources: 521 UNTS 231, Cmnd 4538.
Parties must genuinely consent to marriage and establishes minimum age.

49 *Employment Policy Convention.* 1964. Signed Geneva 9 July 1964 and entered into force 15 July 1966. 70 parties. Sources: 569 UNTS 65, Cmnd 3360.
Parties to promote full employment which is freely chosen.

50 *International Convention on the Elimination of All Forms of Racial Discrimination.* 1966. Signed New York 7 March 1966 and entered into force 4 January 1969. 127 parties. Sources: 660 UNTS 194, Cmnd 4108.
Parties undertake to end all forms of racial discrimination.

51 *International Covenant on Economic, Social and Cultural Rights.* 1966. Signed New York 16 December 1966 and entered into force 3 January 1976. 85 parties. Sources: 993 UNTS 3, Cmnd 6702.
Signatories agree to take steps to ensure the right to work, and adequate social security and education rights.

52 *International Covenant on Civil and Political Rights.* 1966. Signed New York 16 December 1966 and entered into force 23 March 1976. 81 parties. Sources: 999 UNTS 171, Cmnd 6702.
Parties undertake to ensure political, religious and civil rights.

53 *Optional Protocol to the International Covenant on Civil and Political Rights.* 1966. Signed New York 16 December 1966 and entered into force 23 March 1976. 36 parties. Sources: 999 UNTS 171, Cmnd 6702.
Allows individuals to petition the Human Rights Committee alleging breaches of the Covenant.

54 *Protocol Relating to the Status of Refugees.* 1967. Signed New York 31 January

1967 and entered into force 4 October 1967. 94 parties. Sources: 606 UNTS 267, Cmnd 3906.
Extends 1951 Refugee Convention [36].

55 *Workers' Representatives Convention.* 1971. Signed Geneva 23 June 1971 and entered into force 30 June 1973. 41 parties. Sources: 883 UNTS 111, Cmnd 5612.
Protects trade union representatives from discrimination.

56 *International Convention on the Suppression and Punishment of the Crime of Apartheid.* 1973. Signed New York 30 November 1973 and entered into force 18 July 1976. 82 parties. Source: 1015 UNTS 243.
Declares apartheid a crime against humanity.

57 *Protocol Additional to the 1949 Geneva Conventions Relating to the Protection of Victims of International Armed Conflicts.* Signed 8 June 1977 and entered into force 7 December 1978. 55 parties. Source: Cmnd 6927.
Defines international armed conflict so as to include wars of self-determination. See [30–33].

58 *Protocol Additional to the 1949 Geneva Conventions Relating to the Protection of the Victims of Non-International Armed Conflict.* Details as above. 48 parties.
Covers civil wars. See [30–33].

59 *Labour Relations (Public Service) Convention.* 1978. Signed Geneva 27 June 1978 and entered into force 25 February 1981. 17 parties. Source: Cmnd 8252.
Provides for rights of public service workers to organize.

60 *Convention on the Elimination of All Forms of Discrimination Against Women.* Signed New York 18 December 1979 and entered into force 3 September 1981. 85 parties. Source: Cmnd 8444.
Parties undertake to eliminate discrimination against women.

61 *Convention Against Torture and Other Cruel, Inhuman or Degrading Treatment or Punishment.* 1984. Signed New York 10 December 1984 and not yet in force. Source: 6 EHRR 259.
Provides a definition of torture and requires measures to prevent it.

Europe
62 *Convention for the Protection of Human Rights and Fundamental Freedoms.* 1950. Signed Rome 4 November 1950 and entered into force 3 September 1953. 21 parties. Sources: 213 UNTS 221, Cmd 8969, ETS 5.
Initially an attempt by Council of Europe to give effect to ideas incorporated in the

Universal Declaration of Human Rights [86], now the most effective of all human rights instruments. See also [63, 67–71 and 74–76].

63 *First Protocol to the Convention for the Protection of Human Rights and Fundamental Freedoms.* 1952. Signed Paris 20 March 1952 and entered into force 18 May 1954. 21 parties. Sources: 213 UNTS 262, Cmd 9221, ETS 9.
Adds substantive rights to the original Convention. See [62].

64 *European Convention on Establishment.* 1955. Signed Paris 13 December 1955 and entered into force 23 December 1965. 11 parties. Sources: 529 UNTS 141, Cmnd 4573, ETS 19.
Establishes common rules for the treatment of nationals of other member states.

65 *European Agreement on Regulations Governing the Movement of Persons Between Member States of the Council of Europe.* 1957. Signed Paris 13 December 1957 and entered into force 1 January 1958. 13 parties. Sources: 315 UNTS 139, ETS 25.
Provides for freedom of movement of individuals between signatory states.

66 *European Social Charter.* 1961. Signed Turin 18 October 1961 and entered into force 26 February 1965. 14 parties. Sources: 529 UNTS 89, Cmnd 2643, ETS 35.
Promotes economic and social rights.

67 *Second Protocol to the European Convention for the Protection of Human Rights and Fundamental Freedoms.* 1963. Signed Strasbourg 6 May 1963 and entered into force 21 September 1970. 21 parties. Sources: Cmnd 4551, ETS 44.
Gives the European Commission of Human Rights the right to give advisory opinions on legal questions concerning the interpretation of the Convention. See [62].

68 *Third Protocol to the European Convention for the Protection of Human Rights and Fundamental Freedoms.* 1963. Signed Strasbourg 6 May 1963 and entered into force 21 September 1970. 21 parties. Sources: Cmnd 4552, ETS 45.
Amends Articles 29, 30 and 34 of main Convention. See [62].

69 *Fourth Protocol to the European Convention for the Protection of Human Rights and Fundamental Freedoms.* 1963. Signed Strasbourg 16 September 1963 and entered into force 2 May 1968. 13 parties. Sources: Cmnd 2309, ETS 46.
Adds further substantive rights to the Convention. See [62].

70 *Fifth Protocol to the European Convention for the Protection of Human Rights and Fundamental Freedoms.* 1966. Signed Strasbourg 20 January 1966 and entered into force 20 December 1971. 21 parties. Sources: Cmnd 4963, ETS 55.
Amends Articles 22 and 40 of main Convention. See [62].

71 *European Agreement Relating to Persons Participating in Proceedings of the European Commission and Court of Human Rights.* 1969. Signed London 6 May 1969 and entered into force 17 April 1971. 17 parties. Sources: 788 UNTS 244, Cmnd 4699, ETS 67.

Allows freedom of movement and correspondence to individuals participating in proceedings under the European Convention on Human Rights. See [62].

72 *European Convention on the Legal Status of Children Born Out of Wedlock.* 1975. Signed Strasbourg 15 October 1975 and entered into force 11 August 1978. 9 parties. Sources: Cmnd 8287, ETS 85.

Provides for legal rights for children born out of wedlock.

73 *Convention for the Protection of Individuals with Regard to Automatic Processing of Personal Data.* 1981. Signed Strasbourg 28 January 1981 and not yet in force. 5 parties. Sources: Cmnd 8341, ETS 108.

Protects automated personal data files.

74 *Sixth Protocol to the European Convention for the Protection of Human Rights and Fundamental Freedoms.* 1983. Signed Strasbourg 28 April 1983 and not yet in force. 5 parties. Sources: 22 ILM 538, ETS 114.

Signatories to abolish death penalty in peace time. See [62].

75 *Seventh Protocol to the European Convention for the Protection of Human Rights and Fundamental Freedoms.* 1984. Signed Strasbourg 22 November 1984 and not yet in force. Sources: 7 EHRR 1, ETS 117.

Provides for rights in regard to criminal proceedings and in respect of aliens. See [62].

76 *Eighth Protocol to the European Convention for the Protection of Human Rights and Fundamental Freedoms.* 1985. Signed Vienna 19 March 1985 and not yet in force. Sources: ETS 118, 7 EHRR 339.

Provides for a number of reforms to procedures under the Convention. See [62].

Americas

77 *Convention on Asylum.* 1928. Signed Havana 20 February 1928 and entered into force 21 May 1929. 15 parties. Sources: 132 LNTS 323, 133 BFSP 17, USTS 815.

Provides for rights of asylum to political offenders. Amended by 1933 Montevideo Convention [78] and 1954 Caracas Convention [82].

78 *Convention on Political Asylum.* 1933. Signed Montevideo 26 December 1933 and entered into force 28 March 1935. 15 parties. Source: 152 BFSP 231.

Modified 1928 Havana Convention [77].

79 *Inter American Convention on the Granting of Political Rights to Women*. 1948. Signed Bogotá 2 May 1948 and entered into force 22 April 1949. 21 parties. Sources: 27 *US Treaties* 3301, *Pan American Treaty Series* 3.
Provides for political rights for women.

80 *Inter American Convention on the Granting of Civil Rights to Women*. 1948. Signed Bogotá 2 May 1948 and entered into force 22 April 1949. 18 parties. Source: *Pan American Treaty Series* 23.
Provides equality of civil rights for women.

81 *Convention on Diplomatic Asylum*. 1954. Signed Caracas 28 March 1954 and entered into force 29 December 1954. 13 parties. Sources: 161 BFSP 570, *Pan American Treaty Series* 18.
Makes provision for the right of asylum in legations and military establishments.

82 *Convention on Territorial Asylum*. 1954. Signed Caracas 28 March 1954 and entered into force 29 December 1954. 12 parties. Sources: 161 BFSP 566, *Pan American Treaty Series* 19.
Provides that states will admit those suffering from political repression elsewhere. See also [77 and 78].

83 *American Convention on Human Rights*. 1969. Signed San José 22 November 1969 and entered into force 18 July 1978. 19 parties. Sources: 65 AJIL 679, *Pan American Treaty Series* 36, 9 ILM 673.
Provides for human rights in the Americas.

Africa
84 *Treaty of the Economic Community of West African States*. 1975. Signed Lagos 28 May 1975 and entered into force 20 June 1975. 16 parties. Source: 1010 UNTS 17. Protocol relating to free movement of persons, residence and establishment. Signed 29 May 1979.

85 *African Charter of Human and Peoples Rights*. 1981. Signed Banjul 26 June 1981 and not yet in force. 17 parties. Source: 21 ILM 59.
Parallels European and American instruments though with greater emphasis on the individual's responsibilities.

Other Human Rights Instruments

United Nations
86 *Universal Declaration of Human Rights*. Adopted 10 December 1948. UN General Assembly Resolution 217a(III). Reprinted in Djonovich, Vol. II, 1948–9, p. 135, and 43 AJIL Supplement, 1949, p. 127.

87 *Statute of the Office of the United Nations High Commission for Refugees.* 14 December 1950. General Assembly Resolution 428(V). Reported in Djonovich, Vol. III, 1950-2, p. 120.

88 *Standard Minimum Rules for the Treatment of Prisoners.* UN Economic and Social Council Resolutions 663(XXIV) of 31 July 1957 and 2076 (LXII) of 13 May 1977.

89 *Declaration of the Rights of the Child.* UN General Assembly Resolution 1386(XIV) of 20 November 1959. Reprinted in Djonovich, Vol. VII, 1958-60, p. 195.

90 *Declaration on the Granting of Independence to Colonial Countries and Peoples.* UN General Assembly Resolution 1514(XV) of 14 December 1960. Reprinted in Djonovich, Vol. VIII, 1960-2, p. 188.

91 *Permanent Sovereignty over Natural Resources.* UN General Assembly Resolution 1803(XVII) of 14 December 1962. Reprinted in Djonovich, Vol. IX, 1962-3, p. 107.

92 *United Nations Declaration on the Elimination of All Forms of Racial Discrimination.* UN General Assembly Resolution 1904(XVIII) of 20 November 1963. Reprinted in Djonovich, Vol. IX, 1962-3, p. 224.

93 *Recommendation on Consent to Marriage, Minimum Age for Marriage and Registration of Marriages.* UN General Assembly Resolution 2018(XX) of 1 November 1965. Reprinted in Djonovich, Vol. X, 1964-5, p. 132.

94 *Declaration on the Promotion Among Youth of the Ideals of Peace, Mutual Respect and Understanding Between Peoples.* UN General Assembly Resolution 2037(XX) of 7 December 1965. Reprinted in Djonovich, Vol. X, 1964-5, p. 136.

95 *Declaration on the Elimination of Discrimination Against Women.* UN General Assembly Resolution 2263(XXII) of 7 November 1967. Reprinted in Djonovich, Vol. XI, 1966-8, p. 275.

96 *Declaration on Territorial Asylum.* UN General Assembly Resolution 2312(XXII) of 14 December 1967. Reprinted in Djonovich, Vol. XI, 1966-8, p. 321.

97 *Proclamation of Teheran.* Final Act of UN International Conference on Human Rights, Teheran, 13 May 1968. UN Publications E.68.XIV2.

98 *Declaration on Social Progress and Development.* UN General Assembly Resolution 2542(XXIV) of 11 December 1969. Reprinted in Djonovich, Vol. XII, 1968-9, p. 257.

99 *Declaration on the Rights of Mentally Retarded Persons.* UN General Assembly Resolution 2856(XXVI) of 20 December 1971. Reprinted in Djonovich, Vol. XIII, 1970-1, p. 449.

100 *Universal Declaration on the Eradication of Hunger and Malnutrition.* Adopted 16 November 1974 by World Food Conference convened under UN General Assembly Resolution 3180(XXVIII) of 17 December 1973. Reprinted in Djonovich, Vol. XIV, 1972-4, p. 436. Endorsed by UN General Assembly Resolution 3348(XXIX) of 17 December 1974. Reprinted in Djonovich, Vol. XV, 1974-6, p. 325.

101 *Declaration on the Protection of Women and Children in Emergency and Armed Conflict.* UN General Assembly Resolution 3318(XXIX) of 14 December 1974. Reprinted in Djonovich, Vol. XV, 1974-6, p. 396.

102 *Declaration on the Protection of All Persons from Being Subjected to Torture and Other Cruel, Inhuman or Degrading Treatment or Punishment.* UN General Assembly Resolution 3452(XXX) of 9 December 1975. Reprinted in Djonovich, Vol. XV, 1974-6, p. 531.

103 *Declaration on the Rights of Disabled Persons.* UN General Assembly Resolution 3447(XXX) of 9 December 1975. Reprinted in Djonovich, Vol. XV, 1974-6, p. 528.

104 *Code of Conduct for Law Enforcement Officials.* UN General Assembly Resolution 34/179 of 17 December 1979. Reprinted in Djonovich, Vol. XVII, 1978-9, p. 412.

105 *Declaration on the Elimination of All Forms of Intolerance and of Discrimination Based on Religion or Belief.* UN General Assembly Resolution 36/55 of 25 November 1981. Reprinted in Djonovich, Vol. XX, 1981-2, p. 401.

106 *Principles of Medical Ethics Relative to the Role of Health Personnel Particularly Physicians, in the Protection of Prisoners and Detainees Against Torture and other Cruel Inhuman or Degrading Treatment or Punishment.* UN General Assembly Resolution 37/194 of 18 December 1982. Reprinted in Djonovich, Vol. XXI, 1982-3, p. 432.

International

107 *Conference on Security and Co-operation in Europe: Final Act.* Concluded at Helsinki, 1 August 1975. Reprinted in 14 *International Legal Materials*, 1975, p. 1292. Signed by 35 states.
This statement of intent includes an important section on Human Rights and Fundamental Freedoms.

Americas

108 *American Declaration on the Rights and Duties of Man.* Final Act of the Ninth International Conference of American States, Bogotá, 1948. Reprinted 43 AJIL Supplement, 1949, p. 133.

Islam

109 *Universal Islamic Declaration of Human Rights.* 19 September 1981. Reprinted in 4 EHRR 1982, p. 433.

7 Constitutional Protection of Human Rights

This *Keyguide* is concerned with the international protection of human rights, but the extent to which human rights are protected under the constitutional laws of different states is very important to the individual and provides valuable opportunities for comparative study. The subject of the protection of human rights under the constitutional law of the 170 or so states in the world is beyond the compass of this brief *Keyguide* but, for the comparativist, the principal source works on the constitutions of states and a few of the more useful digests and secondary works are listed. Some additional monographs on the comparative constitutional protection of human rights under domestic laws are listed below [479–505].

Principal Sources

110 Blaustein, A. P. and **Flanz, G. H.** *Constitutions of the Countries of the World.* Dobbs Ferry, New York: Oceana, 1965–71. 13 vols.
Looseleaf format which allows updating as new constitutions come into force. The most useful source for world constitutions and an invaluable work for anyone researching into comparative constitutional structures and protections.

111 Blaustein, A. P. and **Blaustein, E. B.** *Constitutions of Dependencies and Special Sovereignties.* Dobbs Ferry, New York: Oceana, 1975. 2 vols.
Looseleaf. A companion series to the above.

112 Peaslee, A. J. and **Peaslee Xydis, D.** *Constitutions of Nations.* 3rd. ed. Hague: Nijhoff, 1965–70. 4 vols in 7.
Now being updated by a revised 4th ed. of which Vol. 1 *Africa* (1974) and Vol. 2

Asia and Australia (1985) have so far been published. This work which dates back to 1950 suffers in comparison with Blaustein [110 and 111] by its lack of frequent updating, although the new 4th ed. will provide texts for most newly independent states.

Digests and Secondary Works

There are many of these and a full listing of texts which provide selected constitutions is not possible. It should be emphasized that the following are merely examples of monographs in the field.

113 Dale, W. *The Modern Commonwealth*. London: Butterworth, 1983. 300 pp.
The first volume in Butterworth's *Commonwealth Law Series* contains a description of the Bills of Rights provisions found in the constitutions of each of the Commonwealth countries.

114 Finer, S. E. (ed.). *Five Constitutions: Contrasts and comparisons*. Hassocks, East Sussex: Harvester, 1978. 349 pp.
Useful and scholarly comparative study of the constitutions of Great Britain, USA, USSR, West Germany and France.

115 Goerner, E. A. *The Constitutions of Europe*. Chicago: Regnery, 1967. 219 pp.
A brief account of the principal constitutional protections in Great Britain, France, West Germany and the USSR.

116 Triska, J. F. (ed.). *Constitutions of the Communist Party States*. Stanford, California: Hoover Institution, 1968. 541 pp.
A little dated, but a valuable reference work to the constitutions of fourteen principal communist states.

117 Wolf-Phillips, L. *Constitutions of Modern States: Selected texts and commentary*. New York: Praeger, 1968. 274 pp.
When it first appeared this was an interesting, though selective, study of the constitutions of China, France, West Germany, India, Indonesia, Japan, Malawi, Mexico, USSR, UK, USA and Yugoslavia. It is now becoming a little out of date.

8 Law Reports

Although a guide to the principal sources of international law cases is provided, the Permanent Court of International Justice (1922–46) and its successor the International Court of Justice (now commonly known as the World Court) have never had compulsory general jurisdiction in respect of international law disputes. So, despite the number of treaties protecting human rights, the international case law is thin; though some important cases concerning the protection of minority rights under the peace treaties of 1919 were heard by the PCIJ.

In contrast, the work of the United Nations is of considerable importance; its literature is listed separately [138–174]. The Council of Europe has built a significant body of case law under the European Convention on Human Rights, and this is noted here. So far, the American Convention has produced little case law, though advisory decisions of the Inter-American Court of Human Rights have appeared and are published in the *Human Rights Law Journal* [265] and the *European Human Rights Reports* [137] as well as being available from the Organization of American States.

International Law Cases

Official sources
118 Permanent Court of International Justice. *Judgments, Orders and Advisory Opinions.* Series A, B and C. Leiden: Sijthoff, 1922–40.
This series was succeeded by the International Court of Justice Reports in 1946. It contains the official and comprehensive reports of all the decisions of the PCIJ, including much of the preliminary proceedings and pleadings.

119 International Court of Justice. *Reports of Judgments, Advisory Opinions and Orders.* Leiden: International Court of Justice, 1947–. Irregular.

As in the case of the PCIJ reports, this series contains the official and comprehensive reports of ICJ decisions.

120 International Court of Justice. *Pleadings, Oral Arguments and Documents.* Leiden: International Court of Justice, 1947–. Irregular.

Only of interest to researchers in depth.

Digests and unofficial series

121 *Annual Digest and Reports of Public International Law Cases.* London: Longmans Green/Butterworth, 1932–. Irregular. From Vol. 17 became *International Law Reports.*

A very useful work, giving more concise reports of World Court decisions and of decisions by arbitral bodies and national courts, etc. More recent volumes of the *International Law Reports* reflect the substantial increase in human rights decisions at international, regional and national level, though the emphasis is principally on topics which are considered more central to international law such as nationality, rights of aliens, extradition, protection of minorities, etc.

122 Hambro, E. *et al* (eds.). *The Case Law of the International Court.* Leiden: Sijthoff, 1952–74. 7 vols in 13.

An important work of reference to the jurisprudence of the ICJ; usefully includes sections on human rights in each volume.

123 *International Law Reports.*
See [121].

124 Whiteman, M. M. *Digest of International Law.* Washington: USGPO, 1963–73. 15 vols.

The last in a series of comprehensive multi-volume digests of the entire range of international law, with emphasis on United States practice. Earlier series were produced by Wharton, Moore and Hackworth but include little of significance to the human rights researcher. Indeed, only a small part of Whiteman's series is relevant. Since 1973 a new series entitled *Digest of United States Practice in International Law* has been produced annually. As its title implies, this concentrates entirely on US practice, but it does include some human rights coverage.

European Convention Case Law

Official sources

125 European Court of Human Rights. Series A. *Judgments and Decisions.* Cologne: Carl Heymanns, 1961–. Irregular.

Provides the official texts of all the decisions and instruments of the Court and is an important library holding.

126 European Court of Human Rights. Series B. *Pleadings, Oral Arguments and Documents*. Cologne: Carl Heymanns, 1961–. Irregular.
Publication is much slower than for volumes in Series A. This series contains the important texts of the pleadings and arguments before the Court. Valuable to the advanced researcher and the practitioner.

127 European Court of Human Rights. *Judgments*. Strasbourg: Council of Europe, 1960–. Irregular.
Judgments are available very quickly in mimeographed form from the Registrar of the Court on application. They are provided free and are a most valuable service to libraries, researchers and practitioners.

128 European Commission of Human Rights. *Collection of Decisions*. Strasbourg: Council of Europe, 1960–74. 46 vols.
A summary of the first thirty volumes was published in 1981. This is a valuable source of information on the practice of the Commission, giving insight into the working of the Convention. Highly selective and produced in mimeographed form, but nevertheless provides a great deal of source material showing cases which have been held to be inadmissible and others admitted together with the supporting opinions of the Commission.

129 European Commission of Human Rights. *Decisions and Reports*. Strasbourg: Council of Europe, 1975–.
37 vols published by early 1987 covering period up to July 1984. A summary and index for Vols 1–20 is available. Replaces the *Collection of Decisions* [128] in a more attractive format.

130 European Commission of Human Rights. *Reports*. Strasbourg: Council of Europe. Irregular.
Some Commission reports appear under this cover title when they are released in mimeographed form following the decision of the Commission without a resolution of the Committee of Ministers. They are available free on application.

131 European Convention on Human Rights. *Decisions*. Strasbourg: Council of Europe. Irregular.
As with [130], these are available in mimeographed form free on application. They tend to appear some time after the Commission has given its opinion and only when the Committee of Ministers has made its recommendation on the outcome of the case.

132 European Commission of Human Rights. *Yearbook of the European Convention* *on Human Rights*. Hague: Nijhoff, 1955/7–. Annual.

Although this series is not confined to law reporting and reference to it is made elsewhere in this *Keyguide* [213], it is worthy of note here as one of the major sources for European Convention case law.

Other European series

133 *Case Law on the European Social Charter*. Strasbourg: Council of Europe, 1982. 164 pp.

A useful work in an area of human rights protection in which the Council of Europe has made less well publicized progress.

134 *Collection of Decisions of National Courts Relating to the European Convention on Human Rights*. Strasbourg: Council of Europe, 1969.

With four supplements covering the period up to 1974. Provides 495 summaries of decisions of national courts of the contracting parties referring to the European Convention.

135 *Digest of Case Law Relating to the European Convention on Human Rights 1955–1967*. Heule, Belgium: Editions Administrative UGA.SA, 1970. 523 pp.

A useful work when it first appeared, this digest is now increasingly out of date. It is still of use in respect of the development of case law in the first decade of the Convention.

136 *Digest of Strasbourg Case Law Relating to the European Convention on Human Rights*. Cologne: Carl Heymanns, 1984–5. 6 vols.

A most important work of introduction and reference for students, researchers and practitioners, covering judgments, reports and opinions up to 1982, cross-referenced to Articles in the Convention and fully indexed.

137 *European Human Rights Reports*. London: European Law Centre, 1979–. Quarterly.

The most accessible of all the source works on the European case law. Decisions of the Court are reported quickly with useful headnoting. A valuable selection of decisions of the Commission is also included as is the text of other human rights instruments as they appear and the decisions (such as·they are) of the Inter-American Court of Human Rights.

There are other sources for human rights case reporting. Many of these are referred to in the periodical and official documentation chapters of this *keyguide*. For example, the *European Law Review* [257] and *Human Rights Law Journal* [265] both carry digests of recent decisions. The Council of Europe produce periodic reviews, such as the series entitled *Stock-taking on the European Convention on Human Rights* [210], which provides easy access to recent developments. Although documentation of cases in the international and European fields is fairly well developed, case law on the American Convention is as yet in its infancy. Official reports are produced by the Organization of American States, but these are not easily obtained, and the general researcher should note that the case digest in the *Human Rights Law Journal* [265] and the *European Human Rights Reports* [137] series carry non-European matter. Finally, it must be remembered that cases with human rights implications may appear in other more general series of law reports than those mentioned above. The reader who does not have access to any of the series noted should also remember that many of the monographs listed below make reference to the more important decisions of the courts.

9 International and Regional Documentation

In this chapter are listed some of the more important materials produced by the main international and regional organizations concerned with the protection of human rights which have not already been noted in the chapters on treaties and law reports.

It must be emphasized that these listings are of necessity selective. Only a proportion of the activities of organizations such as the United Nations and the Council of Europe are concerned with the protection of human rights and much of their documentation is of no interest to the human rights student. Although an attempt has been made to list most of the regular documentary sources and serials relevant to human rights emanating from these bodies, they are by no means all readily available to the researcher. In the case of United Nations publications in particular, distinction must be drawn between sales publications which can be purchased through major booksellers in most countries and non-sales items which are often only intended for circulation within the UN and may not be available to the outside reader. However, many of the reports and series noted here will in fact be available in larger university or national library collections, or may be obtainable directly on application to the organization concerned; the Council of Europe is particularly helpful in this respect.

A further caveat must be introduced. Although major documentary and secondary serial sources emanating from these organizations are listed, it would be impossible to produce a full listing of all the individual studies which they have sponsored. Some of the more important studies are listed in the monograph chapter; this chapter is confined rather to those works which seek to provide a broad overview of the activities of particular organizations or to reprinting some of their more important documentation. For fuller information on the publications of the various bodies, the reader is referred to the short list of major bibliographic sources at the start of each section for the individual organizations.

Although this chapter is concerned with documentation produced by the principal international organizations, the reader will note the inclusion of the occasional commercially produced bibliographical guide and some other commercial publications where these offer a speedy, clearer or efficient alternative source of information.

United Nations and League of Nations

Bibliographic sources

138 Aufricht, H. *Guide to League of Nations Publications: A bibliographic survey of the work of the League of Nations 1920–1947.* New York: Columbia University Press, 1951. 682 pp.

The best guide to League of Nations publications and of value to those researching developments in the inter-war period and in particular to the work of the League in protecting minority rights.

139 *Bibliography on the Protection of Human Rights of Works Published after 1939.* New York: United Nations, 1951. 248 pp.

A useful guide to works published in the 1940s, especially in the period leading up to the UN Declaration on Human Rights.

140 Birchfield, M. E. *The Complete Reference Guide to United Nations Sales Publications 1946–1978.* New York: UNIFO, 1982. 2 vols.

An important guide although it should be noted that many relevant UN documents are not sales publications and therefore are not easily available.

141 *Checklist of United Nations Documents 1946–1949. Part 5: Economic and Social Council.* New York: United Nations, 1949–52. 3 vols.

Covers early UN publications on human rights matters. Forms the first of a series of publications listing and indexing UN documentation. See also [143–147].

142 Hajnal, P. *Guide to United Nations Organization, Documentation and Publicity, for Students, Researchers, Librarians.* Dobbs Ferry, New York: Oceana, 1978. 450 pp.

The best single-volume reference guide to UN documentation.

143 *United Nations Documents Index.* New York: United Nations, 1950–73. 24 vols.

The fullest guide to UN publications for the period. Replaced by *UNDEX* in 1974. See [145].

144 *United Nations Documents Index. United Nations and Specialized Agencies Documents and Publications.* Cumulated Index Vols 1–13, 1950–62. New York: Kraus-Thompson, 1974. 4 vols.

145 *UNDEX: United Nations Documents Index Series, A, B, C.* New York: UNIFO, 1974-8. Annual.
Less comprehensive than the previous series. *UNDEX* was in turn replaced by the more useful *UNDOC* in 1979.

146 *UNDOC: Current index. United Nations Document Index.* New York: United Nations, 1979-. Monthly, cumulating annually.
Comprehensive listing of all UN documents received by Dag Hammerskjold Library. Easier to use than *UNDEX*.

147 *United Nations Document Series Symbols 1946-1977: Cumulative list with indexes.* New York: United Nations, 1978. 312 pp.
Useful for tracing human rights series.

148 Winton, H. *Publications of the United Nations System: A reference guide.* Ann Arbor, Michigan: Bowker, 1972. 202 pp.
Simpler bibliographic guide to UN publications arranged by subject.

149 Yves, V. and Ghebali, C. *A Repertoire of League of Nations Serial Documents, 1919-1947.* Dobbs Ferry, New York: Oceana, 1973. 2 vols.
As with Aufricht [138] of value for research on the inter-war period. Individual League of Nations titles are not listed in this *Keyguide*.

Series

150 *Annual Report of the United Nations High Commissioner for Refugees.* New York: United Nations, 1951-. Annual.
Included in General Assembly Records and an important work of reference.

151 *Bulletin of Human Rights.* Geneva: United Nations, 1978-. Quarterly.
General report of UN achievements in the field of human rights. Replaces *Human Rights Bulletin* [154].

152 Economic and Social Council. *Official Records.* New York: United Nations, 1946-. Annual.

153 General Assembly. *Official Records.* New York: United Nations, 1946-. Annual.
United Nations records, although not readily available, provide a basic source for the human rights researcher.

154 *Human Rights Bulletin.* Geneva: United Nations, 1969-77. Biannual.
Successor to *International Year for Human Rights Newsletter* [156]. A newsletter carrying details of conferences and other current developments. See [151].

155 *International Woman's Year Bulletin.* New York: United Nations, 1975.
General coverage on women's rights within the UN framework.

156 *International Year for Human Rights Newsletter.* New York: United Nations, 1967–9. 8 issues.
Superseded by *Human Rights Bulletin* [154].

157 *Juridical Yearbook.* New York: United Nations, 1963–. Annual.
Contains decisions of UN tribunals and legal opinions of the UN Secretariat.

158 *Objective: justice. A United Nations review dedicated to the promotion of justice through the self-determination of peoples, the elimination of apartheid and racial discrimination, and the advancement of human rights.* New York: United Nations, 1969–. Semi-annual.
Details UN activity against apartheid and colonialism.

159 *Report of the Commission on Human Rights.* New York: United Nations, 1947–. Annual.
Included in Economic and Social Council *Official Records* [152].

160 *Report of the Commission on the Status of Women.* New York: United Nations, 1947–. Annual.
Included in Economic and Social Council *Official Records* [152].

161 *Report of the Human Rights Committee.* New York: United Nations, 1977–. Annual.
Included in General Assembly *Official Records* [153].

162 *Report of the Social Commission.* New York: United Nations, 1947–. Annual.
Included in Economic and Social Council *Official Records* [152].

163 *Report of the Special Committee Against Apartheid.* New York: United Nations, 1969–. Annual.
Included in General Assembly *Official Records* [153].

164 *Report of the Special Committee on the Situation with Regard to the Implementation of the Declaration on the Granting of Independence to Colonial Countries and their Peoples.* New York: United Nations, 1969–. Annual.
Included in General Assembly *Official Records* [153].

165 *Report of the Sub-Commission on Prevention of Discrimination and Protection of Minorities.* New York: United Nations, 1947–. Annual.
Included in Economic and Social Council *Official Records* [152].

166 *UN Chronicle.* New York: United Nations, 1964–. Monthly.

Originally appeared as *UN Monthly Chronicle,* successor to *United Nations Bulletin,* 1946–54, 16 vols and *United Nations Review,* 1954–64, 11 vols. General information on UN activity in all fields.

167   *Unit on Apartheid. Notes and Documents.* New York: United Nations, 1968–.

168   *Yearbook of the International Law Commission.* New York: United Nations, 1949–. Annual.
Occasionally covers matters of human rights interest, but its main direction lies in the codification of international law.

169   *Yearbook of the United Nations.* 1946–. New York: United Nations, 1947–. Annual.
A general survey of UN activities in all fields. Includes a useful summary of human rights activity together with reference to original documentation. The UN *Yearbook* is sufficiently thorough for most research purposes, although unfortunately there is a considerable time lag, extending to two or three years, in its appearance.

170   *Yearbook on Human Rights.* 1946–. New York: United Nations, 1947–. From 1946–72 issued annually, and then to 1977/8, the most recently published, every two years.
Now considerably behind schedule, but nevertheless one of the most useful sources for the human rights researcher. Part one consists of material reflecting national measures and decisions in the field. Part two deals with the work of the supervisory bodies and agencies which have been established under the various international instruments, whilst part three details other international developments and activities in the field of human rights in the United Nations system.

Monographs
As with the other international and regional organizations, it would be impossible to give a full listing of individual human rights studies which have been produced under the auspices of the United Nations, although some of the more important ones are listed in the monograph chapter. This section is confined to collections of documents and the main introductory texts which provide a lead into the subject of United Nations protection for the interested student.

171   *Human Rights: A compilation of international instruments of the United Nations.* New ed. New York: United Nations, 1983. 147 pp.
Contains the full text of 57 international instruments relating to human rights adopted by organizations within the UN system up to the end of 1982.

172   *Human Rights International Instruments: Signatures, ratifications, accessions etc.* (1 September 1983). New York: United Nations, 1983. 28 pp.

Irregularly produced work showing current ratifications of 21 human rights instruments deposited with the UN. Not a sales publication and therefore not readily available. See also *Multilateral Treaties Deposited with the Secretary-General. Status as at 31 December 1984*. New York: United Nations, 1986. 801 pp. Irregular.

173 *United Nations Action in the Field of Human Rights*. 1983 ed. New York: United Nations, 1983. 389 pp.
One of the most useful summaries of United Nations activity in the field of human rights, with detailed references to original documentation. Along with the two *Yearbooks* [169 and 170], one of the best starting points for research in the area.

174 *United Nations and Human Rights*. New York: United Nations, 1984. 268 pp.
Latest ed. of an introductory guide to UN activity produced by the UN Department of Public Information.

UNESCO

Bibliographic sources
175 *Bibliography of Publications Issued by UNESCO or Under its Auspices: The first twenty-five years 1946 to 1971*. Paris: UNESCO, 1973. 385 pp.

176 *UNESCO List of Documents and Publications 1972–1976*. Paris: UNESCO, 1977. 2 vols and *UNESCO List of Documents and Publications, 1977–1980*. Paris: UNESCO, 1984. 2 vols.

177 *UNESCO List of Documents and Publications*. Paris: UNESCO, 1972–. Quarterly with annual cumulations.

Series
178 *Human Rights Teaching*. Paris: UNESCO, 1980–. Biannual.
Bulletin aimed at promoting liaison between those involved in human rights teaching and research.

179 *Report of the Director-General on the Activities of the Organization*. Paris: UNESCO, 1947–. Annual.

180 *UNESCO Chronicle*. Paris: UNESCO, 1955–80. Bi-monthly.
Now ceased publication.

181 *UNESCO Courier*. Paris: UNESCO, 1948–. Monthly.
The two above titles give general information on UNESCO activity and provide useful documentary references.

International Labour Organization

The work of the International Labour Organization, in so far as it is concerned with protecting minimum conditions of work and rights of assembly whilst outlawing discrimination, is of importance in establishing both civil and political rights as well as social and economic ones. Listed here are the more important documentary sources, and elsewhere a selection of monographs on the work of the organization is included.

Bibliographic sources
182 *Chronological Index of Legislation 1919–1978.* Geneva: ILO, 1980. 240 pp.
A straightforward chronological index to ILO legislation.

183 *ILO Catalogue of Publications in Print 1982.* Geneva: ILO, 1982. 324 pp.

184 **Pease, M.** (ed.). *Consolidated Index to the ILO Legislative Series 1919–1970.* New York: UNIFO, 1975. 264 pp.
Indexes the *Legislative Series* [188].

185 *Subject Guide to Publications of the International Labour Office 1919–1964.* Geneva: ILO, 1968. 492 pp.

Series
186 *ILO Information.* Geneva: ILO, 1965–. Bi-monthly.
Provides general news of ILO activity.

187 *International Labour Review.* Geneva: ILO, 1921–. Monthly.
Contains a number of articles of interest to the human rights researcher; see also the quarterly *Social and Labour Bulletin* which has appeared since 1974.

188 *Legislative Series.* Geneva: ILO, 1919–. Three per year.
Provides edited versions of labour and welfare legislation from countries throughout the world. A cumulative index to the series covering the years 1919–75 is available in two vols.

189 *Official Bulletin. Series A: Information on the activities of the International Labour Organization, texts adopted by the International Labour Conference and other official documents.* Geneva: ILO, 1919–. Three times a year.
One of the most useful sources of ILO information, providing news and texts of new conventions.

190 *Official Bulletin. Series B: Reports of the Committee on Freedom of Association of the Governing Body of the ILO and related material.* Geneva: ILO, 1919–. Two or three issues a year.

191 *Report of the Director General.* Geneva: ILO, 1947–. Annual.
A report to the International Labour Conference summarizing developments in the ILO in the year under review.

Monographs
192 *International Labour Code.* Geneva: ILO, 1952. 2 vols.
Combined collection of ILO conventions and recommendations up to 1951. Now rather outdated but a new collection covering the period 1919–81 has been prepared [6].

193 *The ILO and Human Rights.* Geneva: ILO, 1968. 118 pp.
A report prepared for the International Labour Conference.

194 *ILO Principles, Standards and Procedures Concerning Freedom of Association.* 2nd ed. Geneva: ILO, 1978. 25 pp.

International Committee of the Red Cross

The International Committee of the Red Cross is primarily concerned with humanitarian issues, that is the protection of victims of armed conflict, and with humanitarian law. The development of humanitarian law has a separate history from the movement to develop an international protection of human rights, but the subjects are clearly interrelated. Listed here are the major sources of information regarding the work of the Red Cross, and elsewhere is listed a short selection of the principal textbooks and monographs on humanitarian law [521–535]. This section does not purport to offer a guide to the wider subject of the law of war and human conflict which is a separate subject.

Series
195 *International Review of the Red Cross.* Geneva: International Committee of the Red Cross, 1961–. Bi-monthly.
A French language series under the title *Revue Internationale de la Croix Rouge* has been published since 1869. This is the most useful source for current Red Cross activity providing news along with articles and reviews.

196 *Report on General Activities 1947–1948 to date.* Geneva: ICRC, 1949–. Annual.
Annual guide to Red Cross activities and publications.

197 *International Red Cross Handbook: Conventions, statutes and regulations.* 11th ed. Geneva: ICRC, 1971.
A valuable guide to the structure and activities of the Red Cross.

Council of Europe

Bibliographic sources

198 *Bibliography Relating to the European Convention on Human Rights.* Strasbourg: Council of Europe, 1978. 173 pp.

A valuable listing of material emanating both from the Council of Europe and other sources. Unfortunately it is now rather outdated.

199 *Bibliography of the European Social Charter.* Strasbourg: Council of Europe, 1982.

200 *Documentation Sources on Human Rights.* Strasbourg: Council of Europe, 1978. 27 pp.

Lists the main series and collections of human rights material produced by the Council of Europe.

201 *Reports and Documentation Relating to the European Convention on Human Rights.* Strasbourg: Council of Europe, 1976. 10 pp.

Again provides basic information on Council of Europe publications. Students should also note the annual catalogues of Council of Europe publications. Not all documents listed below are on sale, but most are readily available on request to the Council of Europe.

Series

202 *Activities of the Council of Europe in the field of Human Rights.* 1975–. Strasbourg: Council of Europe, 1976–. Annual.

Report by the European Commission of Human Rights to the UN Commission of Human Rights. Originally appeared from 1973–5 as *Communication to the Commission on Human Rights of the United Nations on the Activities of the Council of Europe.* General review of Council of Europe activities in the field. Less detailed than the *Annual Review* [203].

203 *Annual Review: European Commission of Human Rights.* Strasbourg: Council of Europe, 1970–. Annual.

Information on recent Commission activities, together with brief description of cases and summaries of plenary session minutes.

204 *Forum.* Strasbourg: Council of Europe, 1978–. 4 per year.

Continuation of *Forward in Europe.* Magazine providing general information about Council of Europe activities, including those in the field of human rights, for the layman rather than the researcher.

205 *Human Rights Files.* Strasbourg: Council of Europe, 1978–. Irregular.

Series of monographs dealing with particular human rights issues.

206 *Human Rights. Information Sheets.* Strasbourg: Council of Europe. Irregular.
Provide details of developments within the United Nations and Organization of American States, as well as within Europe.

207 *Information Bulletin on Legislative Activities.* Strasbourg: Council of Europe, Directorate of Legal Affairs, 1978–. 3 per year.
Replaces the *Bulletin on Legislative Activities, Legal co-operation in Europe,* and the *Newsletter on Legislative Activities.* Like many other Council publications, this series is available on application free of charge, and although it is not confined to human rights coverage, it does deal with the more important developments in the field.

208 *Minutes of the Plenary Session. European Commission of Human Rights.* Strasbourg: Council of Europe. Irregular.
In mimeographed format. This is for the specialist. Available on application to the Council of Europe.

209 *Press Communiqués. Human Rights News.* Strasbourg: Council of Europe, 1973–. Irregular.
Until 1985 appeared as *Press Releases.* Available on application to the Council of Europe.

210 *Stock-taking on the European Convention of Human Rights: A periodic note on the concrete results achieved under the Convention.* Strasbourg: Council of Europe, 1971–. Annual.
A valuable summary of European action, formerly produced every 2 years, but now annual.

211 *Stock-taking on the European Convention of Human Rights: A periodic note on the concrete results achieved under the Convention. The first thirty years: 1954 until 1984.* Strasbourg: Council of Europe, 1984. 333 pp.
A cumulative review of the achievements of the Convention.

212 *Survey of Activities and Statistics.* Strasbourg: Council of Europe. Annual.
An annual listing of the applications made to the Commission, with division by country of origin, and a note of reports produced. Available on application to the Council of Europe.

213 *Yearbook of the European Convention on Human Rights.* Hague: Nijhoff, 1955–. Annual.
Vol. 1 bears the separate subtitle *Documents and Decisions 1955–56–57.* Although reference to this series has already been made in the chapter on law reports, it should be stressed that the *Yearbook* provides ready access to the other activities of the Council of Europe in the field of human rights and should be regarded as a basic source for the human rights researcher. A shorter summary of information is provided in the *Annuaire Européen* [248].

Monographs
It should be stressed that the following list is not intended to be comprehensive. Hundreds of reports have been produced by the Council of Europe in the field of human rights. The following items are included as providing useful collections of basic documents, or useful summaries of the impact of the European Convention and of the work of the European Commission and the European Court of Human Rights.

214 *Collection of Resolutions adopted by the Committee of Ministers in the Application of Articles 32 and 54 of the European Convention for the Protection of Human Rights and Fundamental Freedoms 1959–1983.* Strasbourg: Council of Europe, 1984. 148 pp.

215 *Convention for the Protection of Human Rights and Fundamental Freedoms. Collected Edition of the 'Travaux Préparatoires'.* Strasbourg: Council of Europe, 1964. 5 vols and index.
Not normally available; however, a reprint has been published by Nijhoff [443]. Collection of debates and working papers which formed the background to the Convention.

216 *European Convention on Human Rights: Collected texts.* Strasbourg: Council of Europe, 1981. 350 pp.
Provides the text of European instruments in both French and English.

217 *Human Rights in International Law: Basic texts.* Strasbourg: Council of Europe, 1985. 261 pp.
Provides the texts of the major international and regional instruments up to 1985. An earlier edition was produced in 1979.

218 *Manual of the Council of Europe: Structure, functions and achievements.* Strasbourg: Council of Europe, 1970.
A valuable source for early developments in the Council of Europe.

219 *Rules of Court: Règlement. European Court of Human Rights.* Strasbourg: Council of Europe, 1965. 55 pp.

220 *What is the Council of Europe doing to protect Human Rights?* Strasbourg: Council of Europe, 1980. 76 pp.
Introductory text for the layman outlining the Council of Europe activities.

Organization of American States and Inter-American Commission of Human Rights

Bibliographic sources

221 *Documentos Oficiales de la Organización de los Estados Americanos. Indice y Lista* and *Lista General de Documentos.* Washington: Pan American Union, 1960–.
Index and general list of documents of the OAS. An English language *Catalogue of Publications* is available on request.

222 *Documentos Oficiales de la Organización de los Estados Americanos. Indice Analitica.* Washington: Pan American Union, 1960–.
Analytical index to OAS documents. See also [331] in the chapter on bibliographies.

Series

223 *Annual Report of the Inter-American Commission on Human Rights.* Washington: OAS, 1976–. Annual.
A report to the General Assembly of the UN which covers the years from 1970. Summarizes Commission activities, resolutions, and the human rights situation in member states. Also notes areas for future progress.

224 *Annual Report to the General Assembly. Inter-American Court of Human Rights.* Washington: OAS, 1983–. Annual.
Provides overview of the activities of the Court in the previous year. Appendices include texts of advisory opinions of the Court.

225 *Anuario Interamericano de Derechos Humanos/Inter-American Yearbook on Human Rights.* Washington: OAS, 1972–. Biennial.
Unfortunately these are very slow to appear. The following have been published: 1960–7, 1968, 1969–70; the first appearing under the title *Organization of American States and Human Rights 1960–1967* [230]. A further volume covering the 1970s is due to appear. The volumes have Spanish and English texts and include essays on human rights in the Americas, and reports and documentation as well as a useful bibliography.

226 *Organization of American States. Legal Newsletter.* Washington: OAS, 1982–. Quarterly.

227 *Report on the Work Accomplished during the Session.* Washington: OAS, 1960–. General report on Inter-American Commission on Human Rights activity.

Monographs

228 *Handbook of Existing Rules Pertaining to Human Rights in the Inter-American System.* Washington: OAS, 1985. 201 pp.

Most OAS documents and regulations on human rights are reprinted in this periodic volume. Also includes a list of OAS publications in the field.

229 *Inter-American Treaties and Conventions.* Washington: OAS, 1980. 306 pp.
Provides information on Inter-American Conventions adopted since 1902.

230 *The Organization of American States and Human Rights 1960–1967.* Washington: OAS, 1972. 657 pp.
The first volume of the *Inter-American Yearbook on Human Rights* [225].

231 *Ten Years of Activities 1971–1981.* Washington: OAS, 1982. 404 pp.
This full survey reviews activities of the Inter-American Commission on Human Rights during the period 1971–81. A bibliography is included. A Spanish edition is available.

Many other documents and monographs emanating from the Inter-American Commission on Human Rights have been published in Spanish.

10 Periodicals

In this chapter are listed those serials which are concerned either primarily or in part with the international or regional legal protection of human rights. Although one or two current awareness services which either provide factual information or summarize the work of international organizations are noted, no attempt is made to list those journals which are produced by the many pressure groups and non-governmental organizations which are active in the field. Some of these publications are significant for the human rights researcher. For example, Amnesty International produce a number of useful periodical surveys and reports. Brief reference to some of the more important of these series will be found in Part III where some of the principal non-governmental organizations active in the field are listed. Whilst mentioning exclusions, it should also be noted that some journals which are primarily concerned with political science or philosophy may include articles of importance to human rights researchers. However, for reasons of space it would be impossible to list them here. Similarly, with few exceptions, journals which are primarily devoted to the protection of rights within one particular country are not listed. A few serials produced by international organizations are included in the chapter on official documents.

For bibliographic sources, the Bowker company is the main publisher and their general titles provide full coverage of human rights journals and annuals, but many of the general sources listed in the chapter on bibliographies also provide lists of the more important human rights serials.

Various indexes provide fairly rapid and comprehensive access to the contents of law journals most of them are listed here. Other more general sources may also prove valuable. One or two of the most important, such as the *Public Affairs Information Service Bulletin* [306], are noted in the bibliographies chapter, but other general sources such as the *British Humanities Index* may occasionally be of value.

General Bibliographic Sources

232 *Irregular Serials and Annuals: An international directory.* New York: Bowker, 1967–. Now annual.
Includes details of yearbooks and other more irregular serials.

233 *New Serial Titles: A union list of serials commencing publication after December 31, 1949.* New York: Bowker, 1950–. 8 issues per year, with past cumulations.

234 *Sources of Serials: International serials, publishers and their titles with copyright and copy availability information.* 2nd ed. New York: Bowker, 1981. 1824 pp.

235 *Ulrich's International Periodicals Directory: A classified guide to current periodicals, foreign and domestic.* New York: Bowker, 1932–. Annual.
A comprehensive 2-volume listing of world serials. Includes many human rights serials produced by non-governmental organizations as well as the legal titles listed here.

Indexes

236 *Current Law.* London: Sweet and Maxwell, 1947–. Monthly.
Summarizes new legal developments in the UK and indexes new articles appearing in British journals. Includes some titles relating to human rights.

237 *Current Law Index.* Belmont, California: Information Access Co., 1980–. Monthly.
Indexes most American legal journals plus a selection of other English language titles. Human rights material is indexed under the heading, 'Civil Law – International Aspects'.

238 *Index to Commonwealth Legal Periodicals.* Halifax: Dalhousie Law School, 1974–81. Monthly.
Indexed a large number of Commonwealth law journals, many of which were not included in the *Index to Legal Periodicals* [240].

239 *Index to Foreign Legal Periodicals.* London: Institute of Advanced Legal Studies in co-operation with the American Association of Law Libraries, 1960–. Quarterly.
Indexes many English and foreign language periodicals relating to international and comparative law and includes reference to a large number of items on human rights.

240 *Index to Legal Periodicals.* New York: Wilson, 1923–. Monthly.
Indexes most of the major English language law reviews, although with something

of a bias towards US titles. Human rights material is indexed under several headings. A valuable library holding.

241 *Index to Periodical Articles Related to Law.* Dobbs Ferry, New York: Glanville, 1969–. Quarterly.

Early years are covered by periodic cumulations. Covers journals not indexed by the *Index to Legal Periodicals* [240], including some important non-legal sources.

242 *Legal Resource Index.* Los Altos, California: Information Access Co., 1980–. Monthly.

Associated with *Current Law Index* [237] and covers a large number of legal and non-legal serials.

243 *Public International Law: A current bibliography of articles.* Heidelberg: Max Planck Institute, 1975–. Semi-annual.

One of the most comprehensive sources for international law including many articles on human rights, these being included as a sub-section of the topic 'Individuals and Groups'.

Periodicals

244 *Académie de Droit International. Recueil des Cours.* Hague: Nijhoff, 1923–. 5 vols a year.

Includes some substantial articles on human rights as, for example, the 1978 colloquy on the right to health.

245 *Africa Contemporary Record: Annual survey and documents.* London: Africa Research, 1968–. Annual.

Useful general survey of national and Pan-African developments including reference to human rights information which may not otherwise be readily obtainable. The series is particularly useful in that it reprints a number of official documents.

246 *American Journal of Comparative Law.* Berkeley, California: American Association for the Comparative Study of Law, 1952–. Quarterly.

Includes occasional articles on the subject of human rights.

247 *American Journal of International Law.* Washington: American Society of International Law, 1907–. Quarterly.

Probably the single most authoritative international law journal. Includes many important articles and useful book reviews in the field of human rights. Also reprints some of the major official treaties and conventions.

248 *Annuaire Européen. European Yearbook.* Hague: Nijhoff, 1955–. Annual.

Includes a brief survey of developments within the Council of Europe relating to human rights and also a few general articles on the subject. The yearbook also contains book reviews and a selective bibliography. However, for fuller European coverage the reader is referred to the *Yearbook of the European Convention on Human Rights* [213].

249 *Annual Review of United Nations Affairs.* Dobbs Ferry, New York: Oceana, 1949–. Annual.
Provides subject coverage of UN activities and reference to original documentation although without full citation. More rapid in publication than the UN *Yearbook* [169].

250 *British Year Book of International Law.* Oxford: Oxford University Press, 1920–. Annual.
Includes a short annual review of decisions under the European Convention of Human Rights as well as occasional articles in the field.

251 *Bulletin of Legal Developments.* London: British Institute of International and Comparative Law, 1966–. Fortnightly.
Brief digest of legal news and developments throughout the world which includes some reference to human rights.

252 *Bulletin of the GDR Committee for Human Rights.* Berlin: GDR Committee, 1973–. Irregular.
Socialist view of human rights issues.

253 *Canadian Human Rights Yearbook.* Ottawa: University of Ottawa and Carswell, 1983–. Annual.

254 *Canadian Yearbook of International Law.* Vancouver: University of British Columbia Press, 1963–. Annual.
Includes occasional human rights articles.

255 *Columbia Human Rights Law Review.* New York: Columbia University School of Law, 1967–. Semi-annual.
From 1967–71 published as *Columbia Survey of Human Rights Law.* Largely concerned with civil rights in the USA, although it sometimes includes comparative studies of rights in other countries. Little on the international protection of rights.

256 *European Law Digest.* London: European Law Centre, 1973–. Monthly.
Provides a digest of recent legal developments in Western Europe. Each issue includes a short section on human rights and reference to decisions of national and European courts on the topic.

257 *European Law Review.* London: Sweet and Maxwell, 1975–. 6 nos per year.

Valuable for its detailed coverage of recent decisions of the European Court and Commission of Human Rights. It also includes commentary on new European treaties as well as more general articles.

258 *Facts on File.* New York: Facts on File, 1940–. Weekly.
Provides a similar service to *Keesings* [277] but with an American slant.

259 *Freedom in the World: Political rights and civil liberties.* Westport, Connecticut: Greenwood, 1978–. Irregular.
Attempts to assess the human rights ratings of individual countries through a survey of civil and political protections in each.

260 *Harvard Civil Rights – Civil Liberties Law Review.* Cambridge, Massachusetts: Harvard University Law School, 1966–. 3 per year.
Civil rights coverage with emphasis on US law and practice.

261 *Human Rights.* Chicago: American Bar Association Section on Individual Rights and Responsibilities, 1970–. 3 per year.
Although largely concerned with US civil liberties, the journal also includes a few short articles on the international protection of rights.

262 *Human Rights Bulletin.* New York: International League for Human Rights, 1945–. Semi-annual.
Formerly *Rights of Man.*

263 *Human Rights Internet Reporter.* Washington: Human Rights Internet, 1976–. 5 a year.
Formerly *Human Rights Internet Newsletter.* Distributed by Human Rights Internet, a body which seeks to provide a widespread dissemination of information on human rights issues. The *Reporter* is journalistic rather than scholarly in its approach but provides access to a mass of information on national and international human rights problems. Includes bibliographies of new documents and publications in the field and provides contents lists for journals.

264 *Human Rights Journal.*
See *Revue des Droits de l'Homme* [282].

265 *Human Rights Law Journal.* Kehl, West Germany: N. P. Engel in association with International Institute of Human Rights, 1980–. Quarterly.
Absorbed *Human Rights Review* [267]. Although the journal contains a few articles, it is chiefly concerned with providing a full commentary on recent developments in human rights. Includes extensive summaries of new decisions and reports as well as reprinting the text of new agreements. There is considerable emphasis on material emanating from the European Court and Commission, but it also

provides coverage of developments under the American Convention on Human Rights which may not otherwise be readily obtainable. The journal is modelled on the twice-monthly *Europaische Grundrechte Zeitschrift*, produced since 1974 by the same publisher.

266 *Human Rights Quarterly: A comparative and international journal of the social sciences, philosophy and law.* Baltimore, Maryland: Johns Hopkins University Press, 1979–. Quarterly.
Formerly *Universal Human Rights*. Includes useful material on the international and comparative protection of human rights. Interdisciplinary approach to the subject with contributions from lawyers, economists, social scientists, philosophers and others. Includes useful bibliographic material.

267 *Human Rights Review*. Oxford: Oxford University Press, 1976–81. 6 vols.
Absorbed by *Human Rights Law Journal* [265] in 1981. The journal contained many valuable scholarly articles on human rights questions, but its notes were sometimes ephemeral.

268 *Index on Censorship*. London: Writers and Scholars International Ltd., 1972–. Bi-monthly.
Particularly concerned with the right to freedom of expression; provides useful journalistic background on the deprivation of rights in particular countries.

269 *Inter-American Law Review. Revista Juridica Interamericana.* New Orleans: Tulane, 1959–66. 8 vols.
Included a few articles on human rights in the Americas.

270 *Inter-American Law Review*. Coral Gables, Miami: University of Miami School of Law, 1969–. 3 per year.
Formerly *Lawyer of the Americas*. Occasional articles on protection of rights in the Americas.

271 *Interights Bulletin*. London: International Centre for the Legal Protection of Human Rights, 1985–.

272 *International and Comparative Law Quarterly*. London: British Institute of International and Comparative Law, 1952–. Quarterly.
Includes a few articles on the subject of human rights.

273 *International Commission of Jurists Review*. Geneva: International Commission of Jurists, 1969–. Semi-annual.
Formed by the merger of the International Commission of Jurists *Bulletin* and their *Journal*. Includes articles reporting on the state of human rights protection in different countries and regions and on the work of the UN and associated agencies. An important work for the human rights researcher.

274 *International Journal of Legal Information.* Washington: International Association of Law Libraries, 1973–. 3 per year.
Formerly *International Journal of Law Libraries.* Includes occasional bibliographic articles relating to human rights as well as useful book reviews.

275 *International Legal Materials.* Washington: American Society of International Law, 1962–. Bi-monthly.
Reproduces most significant international legal documents emanating from bodies such as the UN and Council of Europe and therefore a useful source for the human rights researcher, although its indexing is somewhat sparse.

276 *Israel Yearbook on Human Rights.* Tel Aviv: Tel Aviv University, 1971–. Annual.
Includes various scholarly articles on problems in the field of human rights.

277 *Keesings Contemporary Archives. Record of World Events.* London: Longman Group, 1931–. Monthly.
Valuable survey of world events as reported by serious press outlets. Includes brief factual summaries of major international and national developments with an indication of original sources. A useful index.

278 *Lawasia. Human Rights Bulletin.* Sydney: Law Association for Asia and the Western Pacific, 1982–. 2 per year.
Deals with human rights protection in Asia and the Western Pacific. Includes reports on developments in individual countries and notes on the work of the Association in promoting human rights in the region.

279 *Legal Issues of European Integration.* Deventer, Netherlands: Kluwer, 1974–. Semi-annual.
Occasional useful articles.

280 *New York Law School Human Rights Annual.* New York: New York Law School, 1983–. Annual.
Deals both with civil liberties and the international protection of human rights. Articles, notes and case comments are included.

281 *Revue de Droit Pénal Militaire et de Droit de la Guerre. The Military Law and Law of War Review.* Brussels: Palais du Justice, 1961–. 3 or 4 per year.
Some relevant English language material on humanitarian law.

282 *Revue des Droits de l'Homme. Human Rights Journal.* Paris: Pédone, 1969–. Quarterly.

Articles in English and French on human rights problems. Also provides information on recent documents, conferences, etc.

283 *Rights of Man.*
See *Human Rights Bulletin* [262].

284 *South African Journal on Human Rights.* Braamfontein, South Africa: Raven Press, 1985–. 3 per year.
Largely concerned with internal problems in the field of human rights but does include a few articles of wider interest.

285 *Turkish Yearbook of Human Rights.* Ankara: Institute of Public Administration for Turkey and Middle East, 1979–. Annual.

286 *United Nations Law Reports.* New York: Walker, from 1966. Monthly.
A newsletter providing brief details of cases and other developments in the field of human rights. Has not appeared for some little while.

287 *Universal Human Rights.*
See *Human Rights Quarterly* [266].

288 *Yearbook of European Law.* Oxford: Oxford University Press, 1981–. Annual.
Includes a survey on developments relating to the European Convention and also some useful articles on human rights topics.

11 Bibliographies

This chapter is divided into two sections. In the first are listed general bibliographies and bibliographic sources which provide access to material relating to the international protection of human rights. Most of the bibliographies listed here are chiefly concerned with law, although reference is provided to one or two more general sources which may be useful. It should, however, be stressed that other general bibliographic sources dealing with subjects such as political science and philosophy may also be of value to some students.

In the second part, details are provided of some of the substantial bibliographies which are either entirely devoted to the legal protection of human rights or to some particular aspect of the field, or which, although they are more widely based, provide an extensive listing of human rights materials. Thus, for example, the substantial international law bibliography produced by Delupis [315] is noted since it lists a wide range of human rights sources.

In addition to the materials listed here, it should be noted that the chapter on official documents lists several other important bibliographies, such as those produced by the Council of Europe [198–201]. In passing, it is worth commenting that the researcher who is concerned with such materials should also note the publication catalogues produced by various national government publishers. For example, the annual International Organizations Publications catalogue produced by Her Majesty's Stationery Office (HMSO) lists a number of human rights publications published by different international agencies. Finally, it should also be mentioned that many of the texts listed in the monograph chapter also contain useful bibliographies, although only one [344] is listed here.

General Bibliographic Sources

289 Besterman, T. *Law and International Law: A bibliography of bibliographies.*
Totowa, New Jersey: Rowman and Littlefield, 1971. 436 pp.
Although it lists a number of bibliographies relating to international law and the
practice of international organizations, this work is dated and is primarily of
historical value to the researcher.

290 Besterman, T. *A World Bibliography of Bibliographies and of Bibliographic Catalogues, Calendars, Abstracts, Digests, Indexes and the Like.* 4th revised ed. Lausanne:
Societas Bibliographica, 1965-6. 5 vols.
Too dated to be of any great value to the human rights researcher, since the
literature of the subject has grown very rapidly in the last twenty years. The
supplement by Toomey [312] does, however, list some relevant material.

291 *Bibliographic Guide to Law: 1975-.* Boston: Hall, 1976-. Annual.
Comprehensive bibliography of law books catalogued by the Library of Congress
during the previous year, arranged by author, title and subject. Human rights
material is listed under the heading 'Civil Rights'. This series replaces the *Law
Book Guide* [303].

292 *Bibliographic Index.* New York: Wilson, 1937-. 3 per year, cumulating
annually.
One of the useful indexing tools produced by Wilson. See also [240]. Each volume
lists a number of bibliographic monographs and articles relating to human rights
although, as with a number of other US-produced series, they are indexed under
the heading of 'Civil Rights'.

293 *Bibliographische Berichte. Bibliographical Bulletin.* Frankfurt: Klostermann,
1959-. Irregular.
Each issue includes a number of legal bibliographies in various languages, but this
work is of limited value to the human rights researcher.

294 Dimitrov, T. D. (ed.). *Documents of International Organizations: A bibliographic
handbook covering the United Nations and other intergovernmental organizations.*
London: International University Publications; Chicago: American Library
Association, 1973. 301 pp.
A general bibliography dealing with the use of international documents and their
bibliographic control. Includes a directory of inter-governmental organizations.

295 Dimitrov, T. D. (ed.). *World Bibliography of International Documentation. Vol.
1: International Organizations. Vol. 2: Politics and World Affairs.* New York:
UNIFO, 1982. 2 vols.
Of limited value in this context, although it does include reference to a few items
dealing with the protection of human rights by international organizations.

296 Gould, W. and **Barkun, M.** *Social Science Literature: A bibliography for international law.* Princeton, New Jersey: Princeton University Press, for the American Society of International Law, 1972. 641 pp.

A useful bibliography which provides reference to some of the more important work by social scientists in the field of international law which may not otherwise be familiar to lawyers. Includes reference to a variety of items dealing with human rights problems.

297 Harvard Law School Library. *Annual Legal Bibliography.* Cambridge, Massachusetts: Harvard University Law School, 1961–81. 21 vols.

Before its unfortunate demise in 1981, a most valuable guide to new legal publishing in both monographs and journals. Its subtitle described it as a 'selected list of books and articles received by the Harvard Law School Library' and each volume included an extensive list of new books and journal articles, in various languages, on human rights.

298 Howell, M. A. *A Bibliography of Bibliographies of Legal Material.* Woodbridge, New Jersey: Appellate Printing Co., 1969–72. 3 vols.

299 Hufner, K. and **Naumann, J.** *The United Nations System: International bibliography.* Munich: Verlag Dokumentation and Saur, 1976–9. 3 vols in 5.

One of the most useful bibliographies on the work of the United Nations and its associated bodies. Includes reference to a large number of secondary sources in various languages dealing with human rights.

300 *International Bibliography Publications of Intergovernmental Organizations.* New York: UNIPUB, 1973–. Quarterly.

Each issue includes a short section devoted to human rights publications emanating from intergovernmental organizations with their bibliographic details and a brief abstract of contents.

301 International Committee for Social Science Information and Documentation. *International Bibliography of Political Science.* Paris: UNESCO, 1952–. Annual.

An extensive listing of political science material in various languages which includes some items on human rights. Includes references to books and journals.

302 *Law Books 1876–1981: Books and serials on law and its related subjects.* New York: Bowker, 1981. 4 vols.

The fullest guide, with some US bias, to law publishing for the period, with material on human rights listed under headings such as civil rights and political science–civil rights. The same publishers produce *Law Information* [304].

303 *Law Book Guide. 1969/71–1974.* Berelson, P. (ed.). Boston: Hall, 1973–4. 5 vols.

Supplanted by the *Bibliographic Guide to Law* [291].

304 *Law Information [19xx]: Current books, pamphlets, serials.* New York: Bowker, 1982–. Annual.

Provides annual updating to *Law Books 1876–1981* [302]. *Bowker's Law Books and Serials in Print Update* appearing 10 times a year provides more regular information.

305 Nelson, B. R. *A Guide to Published Library Catalogues.* Metuchen, New Jersey; London: Scarecrow, 1982. 358 pp.

It should be noted that individual library catalogues may be a useful source for the human rights researcher. In the UK, for example, published catalogues are available for significant law collections such as that of the Institute of Advanced Legal Studies and the University of Cambridge Law Library. Readers should also note the useful *London Bibliography of the Social Sciences.*

306 *Public Affairs Information Service Bulletin.* New York: Public Affairs Information Service, 1914–. Semi-monthly with annual cumulation.

One of the most useful current bibliographies in the political field listing a range of materials appearing in books, journals and government documents. Includes reference to many publications both national and international in the field of human rights. A valuable library holding.

307 Raistrick, D. *Lawyers' Law Books.* 2nd ed. Abingdon, Oxfordshire: Professional Books, 1985. 604 pp.

An unannotated legal bibliography arranged by subject which includes a basic list of human rights texts.

308 Robinson, J. *International Law and Organization. General Sources of Information.* Leiden: Sijthoff, 1967. 560 pp.

A useful general guide to the sources and literature of international law although it is not particularly related to the study of human rights.

309 Szladits, C. *A Bibliography on Foreign and Comparative Law Books and Articles in English.* New York: Columbia University Parker School of Foreign and Comparative Law, 1955. 508 pp.

Forerunner of an important series aiming to 'cover all books and articles in the English language dealing with non-common law legal systems and with general subjects bearing upon the comparative study of law'. Little of interest to the human rights researcher in the first volume [but see 310].

310 Szladits, C. *A Bibliography on Foreign and Comparative Law Books and Articles in*

English. [1953 to date]. Dobbs Ferry, New York: Oceana, 1962–. 6 vols.
As human rights have become the subject of increasing attention, so their coverage in this series has become more extensive, although the space accorded to the topic in these periodic cumulations remains relatively limited.

311 Tearle, B. *Index to Legal Essays: English language legal essays in Festschriften, memorial volumes, conference papers, and other collections 1975-1979.* London: Mansell, 1983. 430 pp.
Notes a number of articles on human rights which appeared in collections published during this period.

312 Toomey, A. F. *A World Bibliography of Bibliographies 1964-1974: A list of works represented by Library of Congress printed catalogue cards.* Totowa, New Jersey: Rowman and Littlefield, 1977. 2 vols.
Supplements Besterman [290] and lists a handful of human rights bibliographies.

Human Rights Bibliographies

313 *Checklist of Human Rights Documents.* Buffalo, New York: State University of New York, 1973–6, Nos. 1–24. Then Austin, Texas: Tarlton Law Library, University of Texas, 1976–80.
A monthly uncumulated listing of new materials, monographs, articles and official documents relating to human rights. Unfortunately this useful series has now ceased.

314 Columbia University Center for the Study of Human Rights. *Human Rights: A topical bibliography.* Boulder, Colorado: Westview, 1983. 299 pp.
An unannotated bibliography listing some 2,500 items relating to human rights which were published before the end of 1982. Limited to English language material appearing in secondary sources. Entries are divided by subject and a list of organizations working in the field is appended.

315 Delupis, I. *Bibliography of International Law.* New York: Bowker, 1975. 690 pp.
This important bibliography contains over 40 pages listing books and articles of direct value to the human rights researcher. It is not confined to the English language and, although now somewhat dated, may be regarded as an important starting point for human rights study.

316 Friedman, J. R. and **Sherman, M. I.** (eds.). *Human Rights: An international and comparative law bibliography.* Westport, Connecticut: Greenwood, 1985. 868 pp.
The most essential bibliography for the human rights researcher. Over 4,000 entries divided by subject provide access to books and articles on all human rights

topics and there is also a valuable list of more general sources. The work is not annotated.

317 Garsse, Y. V. *A Bibliography of Genocide, Crimes Against Humanity and War Crimes.* St. Nicolas, Belgium: Studiecentrum voor Kriminologie en Gerechtelijke Geneeskunde, 1970.
A comprehensive, well-indexed guide to a particular human rights problem, although it is now somewhat dated.

318 Granier, J. P. Human Rights and the Helsinki Conference on Security and Co-operation in Europe: Annotated bibliography of United States government documents. In *Vanderbilt Journal of Transnational Law*, Vol. 13, 1980, pp. 529–73.
Of specialist interest only.

319 Greenfield, R. The Human Rights Literature of Eastern Europe. In *Human Rights Quarterly*, Vol. 3/2, 1981, pp. 136–48.
The first of a series of articles by the author dealing with the human rights literature of particular regions. Useful guide both to the general literature of the area and to the problems of particular countries, including reference to bibliographies, indices, dissertations, documents and selectively to books and articles. The following articles [320–322] cover human rights literature of other world regions.

320 Greenfield, R. The Human Rights Literature of Latin America. In *Human Rights Quarterly*, Vol. 4, 1982, pp. 275–98, and Vol. 4, 1982, pp. 508–21.

321 Greenfield, R. The Human Rights Literature of South Asia. In *Human Rights Quarterly*, Vol. 3/3, 1981, pp. 129–39.

322 Greenfield, R. The Human Rights Literature of the Soviet Union. In *Human Rights Quarterly*, Vol. 4, 1982, pp. 124–36.

323 Greenfield, R. *et al.* Bibliography of Human Rights Bibliographies. In **Friedman, J. R.** and **Wiseberg, L. S.** *Teaching Human Rights.* Washington: Human Rights Internet, 1981, pp. 98–134.

324 Gros Espiell, H. *Implementation of United Nations Resolutions Relating to the Rights of People Under Colonial and Alien Domination to Self Determination: A bibliography.* Geneva: United Nations, 1978. 48 pp.
Several useful short bibliographies relating to particular human rights issues such as apartheid or decolonization have been published by the UN.

325 *Human Rights: A study guide for the International Year for Human Rights, 1968.* London: Heinemann, 1967. 220 pp.

326 International Institute of Human Rights. *Selected Bibliography on the International and Comparative Law of Human Rights.* Strasbourg: International Institute of Human Rights, 1973. 11 pp.

327 International Labour Organization. *ILO Human Rights Activities. Select bibliography of works published otherwise than by the ILO.* Geneva: ILO, 1983. 4 pp.
Lists around 50 major studies of ILO activities by various academics. Available on application to the ILO.

328 International Labour Organization. *Select Bibliography of ILO Publications Concerning Human Rights.* Geneva: ILO, 1984. 9 pp.
Lists around 200 relevant items. Available on application to the ILO.

329 *Journal of International Law and Economics,* Vol. 15, 1981, pp. 33–321. Bibliographic Notes.
An exhaustive study of sources in international law which includes reference to monographs, journals and government documents. Includes some material relevant for the human rights researcher although the scope of the article is wider.

330 King, D. B. Legal Literature on International Human Rights. In *Law Library Journal,* Vol. 55, 1962, pp. 111–17.
An unannotated bibliography which is now somewhat dated. It is worth noting that similar short bibliographies have appeared in journals such as *Choice* and the *International Journal of Legal Information.*

331 Library of Congress. *Human Rights in Latin America 1964–1980: A selective annotated bibliography.* Washington: USGPO, 1983. 257 pp.
A selective bibliography listing not only general works but also those dealing with problems in individual countries. Includes material in several languages, and an appendix of human rights organizations is also provided.

332 Merrills, J. G. *A Current Bibliography of International Law.* London: Butterworth, 1978. 277 pp.
Lists a number of relevant books and articles, but mainly of value for tracing materials published during the 1970s.

333 Martin, R. and **Nickel, J. W.** A Bibliography on the Nature and Foundations of Rights 1947–1977. In *Political Theory,* Vol. 6, 1978, pp. 395–413.
An unannotated bibliography of books and articles appearing since the war on the philosophical concepts and foundations of rights.

334 Miller, W. (ed.). *International Human Rights: A bibliography 1965–1969.* Notre Dame, Indiana: University of Notre Dame School of Law, 1976. 123 pp.
See [335].

335 Miller, W. (ed.). *International Human Rights: A bibliography 1970–1976.* Notre Dame, Indiana: University of Notre Dame School of Law, 1976. 116 pp.

The two above bibliographies list over 1,000 books and journal articles but suffer from inadequate subject indexing.

336 O'Connor, B. (ed.). *International Human Rights: A bibliography 1970–1975.* Notre Dame, Indiana: University of Notre Dame School of Law, 1980. 123 pp.

A revision of Miller's 1970–6 guide [335] excluding items emanating from the UN and Council of Europe. Lists nearly 2,500 items, although again subject access is not strong.

337 Reynolds, T. H. Highest Aspirations or Barbarous Acts . . . The Explosion of Human Rights Documentation: A bibliographic survey. In *Law Library Journal*, Vol. 71, 1978, pp. 1–48.

A valuable survey of human rights documentation, especially that emanating from the major international and regional organizations in the field.

338 Schimane, R. and **Rich, R.** *International Human Rights: A selected bibliography.* Los Angeles: University of Southern California, 1979. 81 pp.

Unannotated bibliography of books and articles relating to human rights. No listing of original documents.

339 Schutter, B. D. *Bibliography on International Criminal Law.* Leiden: Sijthoff, 1972. 423 pp.

Lists a number of relevant titles although its main interest lies outside the field of human rights.

340 Schwelb, E. The International Protection of Human Rights: A survey of recent literature. In *International Organization*, Vol. 24, 1970, pp. 79–82.

A short general survey of some of the major books and documents on the international protection of human rights. Now somewhat dated.

341 Smith, L. S. Current English Language Literature on International Human Rights Law. In *Human Rights*, Vol. 4, 1975, pp. 290–4.

Another very brief survey of the field of human rights.

342 *The Third World and International Law: Selected bibliography 1955–1982.* Geneva: UN Library, 1984. 100 pp.

Includes reference to some useful material.

343 Toman, J. and **Huong, H. T.** (eds.). *International Humanitarian Law: A basic bibliography.* Geneva: Henry Dunant Institute, 1979. 59 pp.

A useful specialist bibliography on humanitarian law.

344 Vasak, K. (ed.). Selected Bibliography on International Human Rights Law. In **Vasak, K.** (ed.). *The International Dimensions of Human Rights*, Vol. 2, pp. 688–738. Westport, Connecticut: Greenwood, 1982. 2 vols.

Bibliographies appearing in general texts are not generally listed in this section, but this one is worthy of note since it is particularly extensive. See also [423].

345 Vincent-Daviss, D. Human Rights Law: A research guide to literature. Part 1: International Law and the United Nations. In *New York University Journal of International Law and Politics*, Vol. 14, 1981, pp. 209–320.

The first of a valuable series of essays providing access to a range of human rights documentation and commentaries in the English language. The first article provides reference to general international law materials, both primary and secondary, which may be useful for the human rights researcher. However, the main concern of the article is to provide a general bibliography of human rights materials and items relating to United Nations activity in the field. A large number of original documents, books and journal articles are noted, and in some cases annotations are provided.

346 Vincent-Daviss, D. Human Rights Law: A research guide to the literature. Part 2: International Protection of Refugees and Humanitarian Law. In *New York University Journal of International Law and Politics*, Vol. 14, 1982, pp. 487–573.

The second article in the series is concerned with the international protection of refugees and material on humanitarian law, including the relevant Hague and Geneva Conventions and the work of the Red Cross.

347 Vincent-Daviss, D. Human Rights Law: A research guide to the literature. Part 3: The International Labour Organization and Human Rights. In *New York University Journal of International Law and Politics*, Vol. 15, 1982, pp. 211–87.

The final article in the series provides a valuable overview of literature relating to the International Labour Organization. Unfortunately plans for a bibliographic monograph based on this work have been shelved.

348 Vincent-Daviss, D. *Selected Bibliography on Human Rights.* New York: New York University Press, 1980. 14 pp.

12 Textbooks, Monographs and Collected Essays

Inevitably there are no straightforward, scientific divisions into which books on the international protection of human rights can be placed, but some categorization is necessary given the large number of titles.

Certain divisions do suggest themselves. Obvious categories are books on the protection afforded within the framework of the United Nations, works on the European Convention on Human Rights, and books on the American Convention on Human Rights. One might go further and list works on the African Charter and the Islamic Declaration, but unfortunately there are scarcely any books devoted wholly to these instruments. Indeed, some of the most useful material is in Vasak's two-volume work *The International Dimension of Human Rights* [423] which has to be classed under the heading 'General'. Similarly many books contain essays or chapters on protection under the UN, the ECHR and the ACHR and other topics, inevitably cutting across any division.

In view of these difficulties, some titles have had to be placed into very broad categories. The pattern adopted is as follows:

1. *General*
In this section are included historical, political and philosophical works, collections of essays which range across the subject, and general accounts of the protection of human rights under international law. In order to prevent the user being faced with a lengthy unbroken list of titles, subdivisions have been introduced: (i) for books which are primarily philosophical or sociological; (ii) for those principally concerned with human rights in foreign policy; (iii) for books mainly concerned with international legal issues; and (iv) others.

2. UN and regional frameworks

This section is divided into books which are concerned particularly with the protection of human rights under the framework of the UN, the ECHR and the ACHR. Also included is a separate listing for books on the Helsinki Accord and a short section on Islam. However, the attention of the user is drawn to the fact that many works in the general section contain chapters dealing with these areas.

3. Comparative

Although this *Keyguide* is an introduction to books and materials on the international protection of human rights and not to the protection of human rights under national laws, clearly any student of human rights will inevitably be concerned with the different attitudes, procedures and levels of protection which states adopt in regard to the subject under their national laws. Earlier, a few of the principal reference books and some secondary works on the constitutions of states were listed [110-117] and through those the user can obtain information on the national protection of human rights. In this section are listed some of the more important comparative studies of the protection of human rights under different national laws. Also included are a couple of titles more specifically concerned with the United Kingdom because they deal with the special problem of establishing fundamental rights in a state which has no written constitution.

4. Specific rights

The literature in respect of some rights is quite significant, justifying separate headings. This is especially true of two areas where international protection has a relatively long and very honourable history through the work of the International Labour Organization and the International Committee of the Red Cross. But there are also major bodies of literature on self-determination and development rights in the Third World, on aliens and refugees and on minority groups.

In respect of those individual rights where only one or two books are listed it does not seem sensible to introduce separate headings, so these are listed together in one section headed 'Others'. Again the user should bear in mind that, although there may be few titles on many of the central civil and political rights, many of the books in the general section [349-423] and several works in the section on Europe [440-463] contain detailed discussion of the protection of these rights. The reader should also remember that, although particular rights issues may not have been extensively covered by monographs in the field, they may still have generated substantial literature in journals.

General

Philosophical and sociological

349 Donnelly, J. *The Concept of Human Rights.* London: Croom Helm, 1985. 120 pp.

A doctoral dissertation reviewing the philosophical composition of the human rights idea with copious reference to philosophical and juristic writings which have gone before.

350 Dowrick, F. E. (ed.). *Human Rights: Problems, perspectives and texts.* Farnborough, Hampshire: Saxon House, 1979. 232 pp.
A collection of essays largely adopting a traditional philosophical approach to human rights.

351 Gewirth, A. *Human Rights: Essays on justifications and applications.* Chicago: University of Chicago Press, 1983. 384 pp.
A rather idiosyncratic book in which the author lets his ideas run away with him. The essays range through studiously philosophical reviews of the 'is-ought' problem to human rights and the prevention of cancer.

352 Glaser, K. and **Possony, S. T.** *Victims of Politics: The state of human rights.* New York: Columbia University Press, 1979. 614 pp.
A sociological reflection on ethical and legal aspects of the subject and on group involvement as oppressor and oppressed.

353 Kamenka, E. and **Erh-Soon Tay, A.** (eds.). *Human Rights.* New York: St. Martins; London: Edward Arnold, 1978. 148 pp.
An important collection of essays of theoretical and sociological interest.

354 McDougal, M. S., Lasswell, H. D. and **Chen, L.** *Human Rights and World Public Order: The basic policies of an international law of human dignity.* New York: Yale University Press, 1980. 1015 pp.
The authors adopt a convoluted style with a vocabulary which at times seems almost private but, despite this, the book is a most important contribution to the legal sociology of human rights.

355 Henkin, L. *The Rights of Man Today.* Boulder, Colorado: Westview; London: Stevens, 1978. 173 pp.
A well-written, wide-ranging review of the genesis of the idea of human rights and its meaning in liberal and socialist societies and in international affairs.

356 Melden, A. I. *Rights and Persons.* Oxford: Blackwell, 1977. 263 pp.
A philosophical analysis of the traditionally central issues of legal obligation together with some interesting reflections on conceptual aspects of human rights.

357 Paul, E. F. (ed.). *Human Rights.* Oxford: Blackwell, 1984. 175 pp.
Collection of theoretical essays by various authors, originally published as an issue of the journal *Social Philosophy and Policy.*

358 Pollack, E. H. (ed.). *Human Rights.* Buffalo, New York: Stewart, 1971. 419 pp.

A wide-ranging collection of philosophical papers originally prepared for a conference on the philosophy of law.

359 Rosenbaum, A. S. (ed.). *The Philosophy of Human Rights: International perspectives.* Westport, Connecticut: Greenwood; London: Aldwych, 1980. 272 pp.

An important collection of essays by distinguished international contributors on the foundations, meaning and application of human rights.

Foreign policy issues

360 Falk, R. A. *Human Rights and State Sovereignty.* New York: Holmes and Meier, 1980. 251 pp.

A study of the politics of human rights with chapters ranging from a review of the evolution of US foreign policy to the impact of the Iranian revolution.

361 Hevener, N. K. (ed.). *Dynamics of Human Rights in United States Foreign Policy.* New Brunswick, New Jersey: Transaction Books, 1981. 375 pp.

A collection of essays by a number of distinguished US scholars critically analysing US foreign policy on human rights issues.

362 *Human Rights in United States and United Kingdom Foreign Policy, A Colloquium, Palace of Westminster, November 27–28, 1978.* London: American Association for the International Commission of Jurists, 1979. 66 pp.

The verbatim report of the proceedings which were attended by several US and UK governmental figures. Occasional insight into official attitudes of the time.

363 Lauterpacht, E. and **Collier, J. G.** (eds.). *Individual Rights and the State in Foreign Affairs.* New York: Praeger, 1977. 747 pp.

A collection of essays going beyond the traditional fields of human rights since it includes such issues as diplomatic protection etc., but useful in dealing with the general principles of international law in respect of individual rights.

364 Lillich, R. B. (ed.). *U.S. Ratification of the Human Rights Treaties: With or without reservations?* Charlottesville, Virginia: University Press of Virginia, 1981. 203 pp.

The failure of the USA to ratify any of the major international instruments protecting human rights is a tragedy for that nation and the world. The papers in this volume result from a conference held in 1979 to discuss the USA's failure in this area.

365 Luard, E. *Human Rights and Foreign Policy.* Oxford: Pergamon, 1981. 38 pp.

A slim essay providing an interesting study of the diplomacy of human rights.

366 Mower, A. G. Jr. *The United States, the United Nations and Human Rights: The Eleanor Roosevelt and Jimmy Carter eras.* Westport, Connecticut: Greenwood, 1979. 215 pp.

An important assessment of the work of two powerful advocates of greater US commitment to the international human rights treaties.

367 Owen, D. *Human Rights.* London: Cape, 1978. 154 pp.
An interesting book since it is written by a former Foreign Secretary of the UK. It tackles the problems of human rights in the UK, especially in regard to race relations, and the diplomacy of human rights in the international arena.

368 Rubin, B. M. and **Spiro, E. P.** (eds.). *Human Rights and U.S. Foreign Policy.* Boulder, Colorado: Westview, 1979. 283 pp.
A collection of 21 essays on rights in relation to US policy.

369 Said, A. A. *Human Rights and World Order.* New York: Praeger, 1978. 170 pp.
A collection of essays whose emphasis is principally on aspects of human rights as they impinge on international relations.

International legal protection
370 Berchtold, K. (ed.). *Human Rights in International Law: Collected texts.* Vienna: Verlag der Osterreichischen Staatsdruckerei, 1979. 479 pp.

371 Brownlie, I. *Basic Documents on Human Rights.* 2nd ed. Oxford: Oxford University Press, 1981. 505 pp.
Undoubtedly the most useful and handy collection of international treaties on human rights in one volume. Any serious student of the subject should have his own copy.

372 Buergenthal, T. and **Torney, J. V.** *International Human Rights and International Education.* Washington: United States National Commission for UNESCO, 1976. 211 pp.
An excellent survey of the history of human rights and the activities of the major organizations. The book is particularly geared towards education in the field.

373 Drzemczewski, A. (ed.). *Cases and Materials on Human Rights.* London: Sweet and Maxwell, forthcoming.
A collection of basic materials.

374 *Encyclopedia of Public International Law, Vol. 8, Human Rights and the Individual in International Law, International Economic Relations.* Amsterdam: North Holland, 1985. 551 pp.
Although unfortunately presented in rather a jumbled order, contains valuable up-to-date articles on an exceedingly wide range of issues concerning the international protection of human rights written by various distinguished scholars.

375 Hannum, H. (ed.). *Guide to International Human Rights Practice.* London: Macmillan, 1984. 320 pp.

Compiled under the International Human Rights Law Group as a simple practical guide on selecting and preparing human rights cases with up-to-date information on international; regional and national protections.

376 Joyce, J. A. (ed.). *Human Rights: International documents.* Leiden: Sijthoff, 1978. 3 vols.
Very much a collection of documents for the researcher, the work contains an interesting but selective collection of international documents covering the major instruments, specific issues and the activities of various organizations.

377 Lauterpacht, H. *International Law and Human Rights.* New York: Garland, 1973. 475 pp.
A seminal work, originally published in 1950, by one of the outstanding international lawyers of the time. Although dated, it still represents an important bridging work between the traditional limited interest of international law in the protection of human rights and the major post-World War II developments.

378 Lillich, R. (ed.). *International Human Rights Instruments: A compilation of treaties, agreements and declarations of special interest to the United States.* Buffalo, New York: Hein, 1982. 472 pp.
A collection of some 40 treaties and agreements, concluded under the auspices of the UN, ILO and other bodies, which together form the main body of the international law protecting human rights.

379 Luard, E. (ed.). *International Protection of Human Rights.* New York: Praeger; London: Thames and Hudson, 1967. 384 pp.
Now somewhat dated, but an interesting collection of 12 essays describing aspects of human rights protection.

380 Meron, T. *Human Rights in International Law: Legal and policy issues.* London: Oxford University Press, 1984. 2 vols.
A theoretical collection of essays by major legal scholars including papers on political, economic and social rights, human rights in armed conflict, the various regional protections, race, sex, and religious discrimination.

381 Osmanczyk, E. J. *Encyclopedia of the United Nations and International Agreements.* Philadelphia: Taylor and Francis, 1985. 1059 pp.
Combines much useful background information on human rights and the relevant conventions, including the texts of the major instruments.

382 Ramcharan, B. G. *International Law and Factfinding in the Field of Human Rights.* Hague: Nijhoff, 1982. 259 pp.
A series of studies by leading practitioners reviewing international standards and procedures in the protection of human rights. Something of a pioneering work.

383 Robertson, A. H. (ed.). *Human Rights in National and International Law: The proceedings of the Second International Conference on the European Convention on Human Rights held in Vienna under the auspices of the Council of Europe and the University of Vienna, 18–20 October 1965.* Manchester: Manchester University Press, 1968. 396 pp.

A wide-ranging collection of papers and responses from the Conference participants representing a range of European and American attitudes to the topic. Largely of historical interest now.

384 Robertson, A. H. *Human Rights in the World: An introduction to the study of the International Protection of Human Rights.* 2nd ed. Manchester: Manchester University Press, 1982. 243 pp.

A fairly up-to-date account of the international and regional protections with the texts of several of the main instruments appended.

385 Sieghart, P. *The International Law of Human Rights.* London: Oxford University Press, 1983. 600 pp.

A major work of considerable importance providing a very detailed commentary in which the author reviews the various international and regional instruments, the general principles within which they operate and the procedures for protection available under them, and analyses the substantive rights, comparing the degree of protection offered under each instrument.

386 Sieghart, P. *The Lawful Rights of Mankind: An introduction to the international legal code of human rights.* Oxford: Oxford University Press, 1985. 252 pp.

Introduces the general reader to the nature and content of international human rights law.

387 Sohn, L. B. and **Buergenthal, T.** *International Protection of Human Rights.* Indianapolis: Bobbs-Merrill, 1973. 1402 pp.

A major repository of extracts from international, regional and national case law, intergovernmental correspondence, petitions, League and UN proceedings and international and regional instruments. A book of great value to students.

388 Sohn, L. B. and **Buergenthal, T.** (eds.). *Basic Documents on the International Protection of Human Rights.* Indianapolis: Bobbs-Merrill, 1973. 244 pp.

A companion volume to the above giving the text of all the major international rights instruments at the time of publication.

389 Tardu, M. *Human Rights: The international petition system.* Dobbs Ferry, New York: Oceana, 1979–85. 3 vols.

In looseleaf format. Analyses procedures under which complaints can be made by individuals or groups against state violations of human rights. An important work for students and human rights practitioners.

390 Trindade, A. A. C. *The Application of the Rule of Exhaustion of Local Remedies in International Law: Its rationale in the international protection of human rights.* Cambridge: Cambridge University Press, 1983. 443 pp.

A very detailed analysis of the rationale behind the rule that the individual must exhaust the remedies available to him under his national law before he can seek an international remedy.

391 United States, Congress, House of Representatives, Committee on Foreign Affairs. *Human Rights Documents.* Washington: USGPO, 1983. 700 pp.

Covers US law on human rights, basic UN instruments relating to human rights and documentation of other human rights bodies established by multilateral instruments.

392 Vierdag, E. W. *The Concept of Discrimination in International Law with Special Reference to Human Rights.* Hague: Nijhoff, 1973. 176 pp.

A study of the meaning of the term discrimination in international law, with special reference to its use in various human rights treaties.

393 Weeramantry, C. G. *The Slumbering Sentinels: Law and human rights in the wake of technology.* London: Penguin, 1983. 261 pp.

A rather futuristic book concerned with the problems of law and human rights in consequence of modern technological developments including such subjects as organ transplants, testing drugs, pollution of outer space and unemployment.

Others

394 Campbell, T. et al. (eds.). *Human Rights: From rhetoric to reality.* Oxford: Blackwell, 1986. 262 pp.

A series of 11 essays, tackling the problem of translating the idea of human rights into a practical response to human needs. Essays on such topics as women's rights, the mentally ill, public assembly, trade unions, and the Third World.

395 Chafee, Z. (ed.). *Documents on Fundamental Human Rights: The Anglo-American Tradition.* New York: Atheneum, 1963. 2 vols.

396 Cranston, M. W. *What are Human Rights?* London: Bodley Head, 1973. 170 pp.

A short, easily read, analytical introduction to the principal human rights with the texts of four major instruments.

397 Dominguez, J. I. et al. *Enhancing Global Human Rights.* New York: McGraw-Hill, 1979. 270 pp.

A review of human rights violations and achievements with principal emphasis on the Western hemisphere.

398 Drost, P. N. *Human Rights as Legal Rights: The realization of individual human rights in positive international law. General discussion and tentative suggestions on an international system of human rights.* Leiden: Sijthoff, 1965. 272 pp.
Somewhat dated now, Drost sets out his own individual programme for the development of human rights protection. It is a work of advocacy and somewhat individual.

399 Ganji, M. *International Protection of Human Rights.* Geneva: Droz, 1962. 317 pp.
Principally of value for its historical account of the development of human rights protections from the second half of the 19th century through to the Universal Declaration and the European Convention.

400 Halász, J. (ed.). *Socialist Concept of Human Rights.* Budapest: Akadémiai Kiadó, 1966. 309 pp.
One of the few volumes in English attempting to explain the socialist theory of human rights and duties.

401 Henkin, A. H. (ed.). *Human Dignity: The internationalization of human rights.* Alphen aan den Rijn, Netherlands: Sijthoff and Noordhoff, 1979. 203 pp.
A collection of essays concerned principally with the traditional civil and political liberties and reviewing the development of traditional ideas into their formulation in the Universal Declaration and the International Covenants.

402 Hersch, J. (ed.). *Birthright of Man.* Paris: UNESCO, 1969. 591 pp.
A source book of statements, extracts and citations on human rights.

403 *Human Rights in a One Party State.* Tunbridge Wells, Kent: Search Press and the International Commission of Jurists, 1978. 142 pp.
A collection of papers resulting from an ICJ seminar concerned predominantly with issues of civil rights. Some useful African contributions.

404 Joyce, J. A. *The New Politics of Human Rights.* London: Macmillan, 1978. 305 pp.
A book for the non-lawyer written by a determined humanitarian reviewing the development of the human rights movement and its impact in the modern world.

405 Laquer, W. and **Rubin, B.** (eds.). *The Human Rights Reader.* New York: New American Library, 1979. 375 pp.
An interesting and wide-ranging source-book for the student with nearly 100 extracts from writings, speeches and constitutional and international documents, historical and modern. Includes a useful bibliography.

406 Lauterpacht, H. *An International Bill of the Rights of Man.* New York: Columbia University Press, 1945. 230 pp.

A powerfully argued case for international human rights protection with the author's own suggested draft code. An important contribution to the thought which motivated the Universal Declaration of 1948.

407 Macdonald, R. St. J., Johnston, D. M. and **Morris, G. L.** (eds.). *The International Law and Policy of Human Welfare.* Alphen aan den Rijn, Netherlands: Sijthoff and Noordhoff, 1979. 690 pp.

A collection of 25 essays concerned with human rights, national developments and social welfare, organized so as to draw attention to the institutional developments of international human rights protection.

408 Macfarlane, L. J. *The Theory and Practice of Human Rights.* London: Maurice Temple Smith, 1985. 193 pp.

A very readable introduction to the principal heads of human rights; especially useful to the general reader.

409 Melden, A. I. *Human Rights.* Belmont, California: Wadsworth, 1970. 152 pp.

An elementary reader reproducing 7 essays by authors including John Locke and Bentham and 4 major instruments including the Virginia Declaration of 1776 and the Universal Declaration of 1948. A work for schools or first-year college students.

410 Moskowitz, M. *International Concern with Human Rights.* Leiden: Sijthoff and Noordhoff, 1974. 239 pp.

A powerful appeal for concrete activity to improve the human position.

411 Moskowitz, M. *The Politics and Dynamics of Human Rights.* Dobbs Ferry, New York: Oceana, 1968. 283 pp.

The content of this book is very political. It is concerned with themes of nationalism, international co-operation, population growth, colour barriers and the North–South divide.

412 Nanda, V. P., Scarritt, J. R. and **Shepherd, G. W.** (eds.). *Global Human Rights: Public policies, comparative measures and NGO strategies.* Boulder, Colorado: Westview, 1981. 318 pp.

A collection of papers by US scholars committed to the defence and development of human rights on a world scale. Contains some powerfully argued papers.

413 Nelson, J. L. and **Green, V.** (eds.). *International Human Rights: Contemporary issues.* Standfordville, New York: Human Rights Publishing Group, 1980. 350 pp.

Discusses some of the cultural and racial issues in the field.

414 Newberg, P. R. (ed.). *The Politics of Human Rights.* New York: New York University Press, 1981. 256 pp.

An interesting collection of essays on theoretical and practical aspects of human rights protection including some very interesting studies of problems in the under-developed world.

415 Plattner, M. F. (ed.). *Human Rights in Our Time: Essays in memory of Victor Baras.* Boulder, Colorado: Westview, 1984. 161 pp.

A wide-ranging series of essays dealing with philosophical and practical aspects of human rights protection.

416 Power, J. *Amnesty International.* Oxford: Pergamon, 1981. 128 pp.

A probing study of the work of one of the major non-governmental organizations concerned with the protection of human rights, illustrated by a detailed review of human rights problems in nine countries.

417 Ramcharan, B. G. (ed.). *Human Rights: Thirty years after the Universal Declaration.* Hague: Nijhoff, 1979. 279 pp.

An important collection of essays reviewing the progress of human rights in the 30 years following the adoption of the Universal Declaration in 1948 and making suggestions for further development.

418 Schwab, P. and **Pollis, A.** (eds.). *Towards a Human Rights Framework.* New York: Praeger, 1982. 258 pp.

A collection of studies intended to develop a framework for the analysis of human rights.

419 Stormorken, B. *Huridocs Standard Formats for the Recording and Exchange of Information on Human Rights.* Dordrecht: Nijhoff, 1985. 112 pp.

A practical guide for human rights organizations to standardize information recording and facilitate the exchange of information in a more reliable and systematic way.

420 Union of International Organizations. *Encyclopaedia of World Problems and Human Potential.* London: Saur, 1986. 1400 pp.

Compiled by the Union of International Organizations, this book provides comprehensive information on a wide range of world problems including denials of human rights.

421 UNESCO. *Human Rights: Comments and interpretations. A symposium edited by UNESCO.* Westport, Connecticut: Greenwood, 1973. 287 pp.

422 Vallat, F. (ed.). *An Introduction to the Study of Human Rights.* London: Europa, 1972. 127 pp.

A collection of essays of wide-ranging interest including historical and social aspects of human rights.

423 Vasak, K. (ed.). *The International Dimensions of Human Rights.* Westport, Connecticut: Greenwood, 1982. 2 vols.
Originally published in French by UNESCO in 1978 under the title *Les Dimensions Internationales des Droits de l'Homme.* Vasak is a leading commentator in the field, although much of his work is not available in English. A major collection of important essays by a number of international scholars, the 2 vols. cover a wide range of topics including regional aspects of the subject in Africa, Asia and the Islamic World.

United Nations and Regional Frameworks etc.

The United Nations and associated agencies

424 Carey, J. *UN Protection of Civil and Political Rights.* Syracuse, New York: Syracuse University Press, 1970. 205 pp.
A realistic appraisal of the UN achievements in the fields of civil and political rights during its first 20 years.

425 Chakravarti, R. *Human Rights and the United Nations.* Calcutta: Progressive, 1958. 218 pp.
A work of significance in illustrating both the extent to which UN protection of human rights was seen to extend in the 1950s and attitudes towards its work.

426 Clark, R. S. *A United Nations High Commissioner for Human Rights.* Hague: Nijhoff, 1972. 186 pp.
A review of the debate which surrounded the proposals for a UN High Commissioner for Human Rights.

427 Daes, E-I. A. *The Individual's Duties to the Community and the Limitations on Human Rights and Freedoms Under Article 29 of the Universal Declaration of Human Rights.* New York: United Nations, 1982. 214 pp.
A study of the role of the individual in preserving human rights.

428 Faundez, L. H. *The Reporting System on the Civil and Political Rights Covenant.* Cambridge, Massachusetts: Harvard Law School, 1979. 123 pp.

429 Henkin, L. (ed.). *The International Bill of Rights: The covenant on civil and political rights.* New York: Columbia University Press, 1981. 523 pp.
An important collection of essays analysing the International Covenant on Civil and Political Rights.

430 **Holborn, L. W.** *Refugees, a Problem of Our Time. The Work of the United Nations High Commissioner for Refugees 1951–1972.* Metuchen, New Jersey: Scarecrow, 1975. 2 vols.
A major study of the work of the UNCHR and the post-war refugee problem.

431 *International Human Rights Instruments of the United Nations 1948–1982.* London: Mansell, 1984. 190 pp.
Attractively produced, useful compilation of all the main instruments on human rights from the UN. This is the most easily accessible source of UN instruments.

432 **Khare, S. C.** *Human Rights and the United Nations.* New Delhi: Metropolitan Books, 1977. 381 pp.
A useful work providing a wider perspective on UN human rights protection.

433 **Lerner, N.** *The UN Convention on the Elimination of all Forms of Racial Discrimination.* 2nd ed. Alphen aan den Rijn, Netherlands: Sijthoff, 1980. 259 pp.
A concise commentary on the text of the Convention.

434 **Lillich, R. B.** *Humanitarian Intervention and the United Nations.* Charlottesville, Virginia: University of Virginia Press, 1973. 240 pp.
A somewhat disjointed book, being the edited record of conference proceedings, but valuable because of the importance of its subject matter. Does international law allow states to intervene in the affairs of other nations for humanitarian reasons, or is it prevented by Article 2 (4) of the UN Charter?

435 **Moskowitz, M.** *Human Rights and World Order: The struggle for human rights in the United Nations.* Dobbs Ferry, New York: Oceana, 1959. 239 pp.
Now of historical interest, but still a useful text on the issues and difficulties in the development of human rights protection in the UN as seen in the late 1950s.

436 **Mower, G. A.** *International Co-operation for Social Justice: Global and regional protection of economic/social rights.* Westport, Connecticut: Greenwood, 1985. 288 pp.
Principally focused on the ICESCR, the book discusses modern attempts to improve and protect economic and social rights.

437 **Ramcharan, B. G.** *Humanitarian Good Offices in International Law: Good offices of the United Nations Secretary General in the field of human rights.* Hague: Nijhoff, 1983. 232 pp.
An examination of the work of the UN Secretary General and of the UNHCHR proposals, with case studies on Bangladesh, S.E. Asia, Cyprus and Iran.

438 **Sohn, L. B.** *United Nations and Human Rights.* New York: Commission to Study the Organization of Peace, 1968. 239 pp.

439 Zuijdwijk, T. J. M. *Petitioning the United Nations: A study in human rights.* New York: St. Martins; Aldershot, Hampshire: Gower, 1982. 397 pp.

A scholarly and informative study of the procedures adopted within the UN for dealing with human rights petitions.

Europe

440 Alderson, J. *Human Rights and the Police.* Strasbourg: Council of Europe, 1984. 214 pp.

A valuable study by a distinguished former UK Chief Constable showing how the European Convention impinges on police procedures and practices.

441 Beddard, R. *Human Rights and Europe: A study of the machinery of human rights protection of the Council of Europe.* 2nd ed. London: Sweet and Maxwell, 1980. 217 pp.

A clearly written, short general introduction to the European Convention and its procedures.

442 Castberg, F. *The European Convention on Human Rights.* Leiden: Sijthoff; Dobbs Ferry, New York: Oceana, 1974. 198 pp.

Originally written in Norwegian, the English version is now somewhat dated in view of the substantial developments in the jurisprudence of the Convention. However, the text still provides a very clear and sound introduction to the principles of the Convention and its procedures.

443 *Collected Edition of the 'Travaux Préparatoires' of the European Convention on Human Rights.* Hague: Nijhoff, 1975–84. 8 vols.

A major source of information for those researching into the background politics and legal issues in the drafting of the Convention.

444 Drzemczewski, A. *European Human Rights Convention in Domestic Law: A comparative study.* London: Oxford University Press, 1983. 394 pp.

An excellent study of the way in which the member states of the Council of Europe provide to varying degrees for the incorporation of their obligations under the European Convention into their internal law.

445 *The European Convention on Human Rights.* London: British Institute of International and Comparative Law, 1965. 106 pp.

A collection of papers by a number of distinguished scholars showing the development of the European Convention as it stood in 1965.

446 Fawcett, J. E. *The Application of the European Convention on Human Rights.* Oxford: Clarendon Press, 1969. 368 pp.

Now out of date, although a second edition is due for publication in 1987, but a most important account of the developing practice of the European Court and Commission. The author is a former president of the Commission.

447 Furmston, M. P., Kerridge, R. and **Sufrin, B. S.** (eds.). *The Effect on English Domestic Law of Membership of the European Communities and of Ratification of the European Commission on Human Rights.* Hague: Nijhoff, 1983. 436 pp.

As its title suggests, this collection of essays is largely of interest to the English reader, but it contains interesting material on the interrelationship of national law and the international obligations of the state.

448 Harris, D. *The European Social Charter.* Charlottesville, Virginia: University Press of Virginia, 1984. 345 pp.

A most important study of the European Social Charter whose significance in terms of regional protection has often been overlooked.

449 *Human Rights of Aliens in Europe: Proceedings of the colloquy held at Funchal-Madeir, October 1983.* Dordrecht: Nijhoff, 1985. 484 pp.

Useful discussion of the problems faced by migrants, be they workers or refugees or their families or others. The issues are particularly significant for many of the member states of the Council of Europe and the European Community.

450 Jacobs, F. G. *The European Convention on Human Rights.* Oxford: Clarendon Press, 1975. 286 pp.

A very readable and sound general textbook on the European Convention, now somewhat outdated, but still of value.

451 Jacobs, F. G. (ed.). *European Law and the Individual.* Amsterdam: North Holland, 1976. 211 pp.

Includes essays on the European Social Charter and the protection of fundamental rights in the European Community.

452 Jacobs, F. G. and **Durand, A.** *References to the European Court: Practice and procedure.* London: Butterworth, 1975. 145 pp.

A useful work for European lawyers and others appearing before the European Court of Human Rights. There have been procedural changes since it was published.

453 Miehsler, H. and **Petzold, H.** (eds.). *European Convention on Human Rights: Texts and documents.* Cologne: Carl Heymanns, 1982. 2 vols.

Texts of the European Convention on Human Rights, its protocols, rules of procedure and of decisions, declarations, resolutions and recommendations of the Committee of Ministers and the Council of Europe.

454 Mikaelson, L. *European Protection of Human Rights: The practice and procedure of the European Commission of Human Rights on the admissibility of applications from individuals and states.* Alphen aan den Rijn, Netherlands: Sijthoff, 1980. 273 pp.

A useful study of the European Commission's practice in respect of receiving and considering applications from individuals and states.

455 Morrison, C. C. *The Developing European Law of Human Rights.* Leiden: Sijthoff, 1967. 213 pp.
An interesting, but rather selective, account of the developing European law of human rights, now overtaken by the author's later work [456].

456 Morrison, C. C. *The Dynamics of Development in the European Human Rights Convention System.* Hague: Nijhoff, 1981. 176 pp.
An interesting, but selective, view of the way in which the European Court of Human Rights has given an extended and dynamic interpretation of many articles of the European Convention.

457 Nedjati, Z. M. *Human Rights Under the European Convention.* Amsterdam: North Holland, 1978. 298 pp.
Offers a detailed analysis of the way the European Court and Commission interpret the provisions of the European Convention. It contains some useful material giving detailed illustration, but the very nature of the study means it is already becoming out of date.

458 Petzold, H. *The European Convention on Human Rights: Cases and materials.* 4th ed. Cologne: Carl Heymanns, 1981. 419 pp.
A collection of materials from the judgments and opinions of the European Court and Commission principally for students.

459 Robertson, A. H. *Human Rights in Europe.* 2nd ed. Manchester: Manchester University Press, 1977. 329 pp.
A very readable book by an author who is a former Director of Human Rights at the Council of Europe. This work is especially valuable in outlining the procedure of the Commission and the Court.

460 Toth, A. G. *Legal Protection of Individuals in the European Communities. Vol. 1: Individual and Community Law. Vol. 2: Remedies and Procedures.* Amsterdam: North Holland, 1978. 2 vols.
A very full study of the protection afforded to the individual under the law of the European Community.

461 Van Dijk, P. and **Van Hoof, F.** *Theory and Practice of the European Convention on Human Rights.* Deventer, Netherlands: Kluwer, 1984. 526 pp.
Originally published in Dutch, the English edition, an updated version of the work, contains a substantial analysis of the procedures under the Convention and of its substantive provisions. A valuable and practical work.

462 Vasak, K. *La Convention Européenne des Droits de l'Homme.* Paris: Libraire Générale de Droit et de Jurisprudence, 1964. 327 pp.

An interesting early work on the European Convention on Human Rights, descriptive and critical.

463 Weil, G. L. *The European Convention on Human Rights: Background, development and prospects.* Leiden: Sijthoff, 1963. 260 pp.

A descriptive and analytical account of the European Convention as it appeared in the early 1960s.

Americas

464 Buergenthal, T. and **Norris, R. E.** *Human Rights: The Inter-American System.* Dobbs Ferry, New York: Oceana, 1982–3. 3 vols. Looseleaf.

An essential repository of source material for any student of human rights. Contains text and commentary on the institutions, instruments, regulations and decisions of the Inter-American Court and Commission. No library should be without this work.

465 Buergenthal, T., Norris, R. and **Shelton, D.** *Protecting Human Rights in the Americas.* Kehl, West Germany: N. P. Engel, 1982. 337 pp.

Described as the first textbook on the Inter-American system to appear since the American Convention came into effect, the book is not a textbook, but a not altogether well-structured collection of quotations from international documents, reports of international bodies and reports of the Inter-American Commission.

466 Inter-American Bar Foundation. *The Legal Protection of Human Rights in the Western Hemisphere.* Washington: Inter-American Bar Foundation, 1978. 118 pp.

467 LeBlanc, L. J. *The OAS and the Promotion and Protection of Human Rights.* Hague: Nijhoff, 1977. 179 pp.

Revised version of author's Ph.D. thesis on the subject of the Inter-American Commission of Human Rights.

468 Schreiber, A. P. *Inter-American Commission on Human Rights.* Leiden: Sijthoff, 1970. 187 pp.

Primarily of historical interest since it predates the entry into force of the ACHR, but still of considerable interest especially in surveying the development of the Inter-American procedures for protecting human rights and detailing comparisons with the European Commission.

469 Vasak, K. *La Commission Interaméricaine des Droits de l'Homme.* Paris: Libraire Générale de Droit et de Jurisprudence, 1968. 287 pp.

An early study of the Inter-American system by a leading human rights expert.

Islam

470 Haider, S. M. (ed.). *Islamic Concept of Human Rights.* Lahore: Book House, 1978. 314 pp.

471 International Commission of Jurists. *Human Rights in Islam.* Geneva: International Commission of Jurists, 1982. 95 pp.

A short report of a seminar on human rights in Islam staged by the ICJ, University of Kuwait and the Union of Arab Lawyers in 1980, providing a brief outline of the Islamic protection of rights in different fields.

472 Khan, M. Z. *Islam and Human Rights.* London: London Mosque, 1970. 146 pp.

Helsinki Accord

473 Bloed, A. and **Van Dijk, P.** (eds.). *Essays on Human Rights in the Helsinki Process.* Hague: Nijhoff, 1985. 285 pp.

Human rights issues in the context of East–West dialogue in Europe. A collection of papers concerned with a range of human rights both socio-economic and political.

474 Buergenthal, T. (ed.). *Human Rights, International Law and the Helsinki Accord.* Montclair, New Jersey: Allenheld Osmun, 1979. 203 pp.

A collection of papers analysing the potential impact of the Final Act of the Helsinki Conference on Human Rights.

475 Chossudovsky, E. *The Helsinki Final Act Viewed in the United Nations Perspective: An essay in the process of detente.* New York: UNITAR, 1980.

Analyses the connections between the Helsinki Conference and the United Nations. Also considers the UN role in promoting co-operation between states with different economic and social systems.

476 Dominick, M. F. (ed.). *Human Rights and the Helsinki Accord.* Buffalo, New York: Hein, 1981. 411 pp.

A symposium reviewing the impact of the Final Act of the Helsinki Conference.

477 Kavass, I. and **Granier, J. P.** (eds.). *Human Rights, European Politics and the Helsinki Accord: The documentary evolution of the Conference on Security and Co-operation in Europe 1973–1975.* Buffalo, New York: Hein, 1981. 6 vols.

A major collection of records documenting the discussions leading to the Helsinki Accord.

478 Kavass, I. I. and **Granier, J.** (eds.). *Human Rights, The Helsinki Accords and the United States: Selected Executive and Congressional documents.* Series 1–3. Buffalo, New York: Hein, 1982. 9 vols.

A collection of documents outlining the impact of the Helsinki Accord on the USA.

Comparative Works

479 Anderson, N. *Liberty, Law and Justice.* London: Stevens, 1978. 140 pp.
An interesting discussion at a broad general level of human rights procedures, race and sex discrimination and freedom of speech etc. by a noted comparative common lawyer.

480 Andrews, J. A. (ed.). *Human Rights in Criminal Procedure: A comparative study.* Hague: Nijhoff, 1981. 452 pp.
Essays on human rights protection for the criminal defendant under the European Convention and in the national laws of North America and Western Europe.

481 Barendt, E. *Freedom of Speech.* Oxford: Clarendon Press, 1985. 314 pp.
A comparative study of the law protecting freedom of speech in the UK, USA and West Germany under the European Convention.

482 Bridge, J. W. (ed.). *Fundamental Rights: A volume of essays to commemorate the 50th anniversary of the founding of the Law School in Exeter 1923–1973.* London: Sweet and Maxwell, 1973. 324 pp.
A collection of essays devoted variously to fundamental rights under English law and in international law with particular reference to Europe.

483 Castberg, F. *Freedom of Speech in the West: A comparative study of public law in France, the United States and Germany.* New York: Oceana, 1960. 475 pp.
A comparative analysis of the right to freedom of speech in France, USA and West Germany written with an emphasis on the historical development of the concept in each jurisdiction.

484 Claude, R. P. (ed.). *Comparative Human Rights.* Baltimore: Johns Hopkins University Press, 1976. 410 pp.
A valuable collection of essays by different authors on the legal development of human rights and comparative aspects of human rights protection in several different states in Asia, Europe and the Americas.

485 Cohen, E. R. *Human Rights in the Israeli Occupied Territories 1967–1982.* Manchester: Manchester University Press, 1985. 300 pp.
A major study illustrating Israeli preoccupation with the problems of human rights in circumstances of belligerent occupation.

486 Duchacek, I. D. *Rights and Liberties in the World Today: Constitutional promise and reality.* Santa Barbara, California: ABC-Clio, 1973. 269 pp.

A comparative examination of the constitutional protection afforded to citizens of over 100 countries and the ways in which this protection is or is not effected in practice.

487 Ezejiofor, G. O. *Protection of Human Rights Under the Law.* London: Butterworth, 1964. 292 pp.
An out-of-date work which ambitiously described the development of human rights as a concept and as a thing of legal consequence in international law and under the European and American Conventions. Interesting sections on the protection of human rights in the British Commonwealth in the 1960s.

488 Franck, T. M. *Comparative Constitutional Process. Cases and Materials. Fundamental Rights in the Common Law of Nations.* New York: Praeger, 1968. 595 pp.
A substantial collection of extracts from constitutions, ordinances, court judgments and other sources from a very wide range of common law jurisdictions. Something of a period piece now since the laws of the former British colonies have developed greatly since 1968 but still provides interesting comparative material on civil rights.

489 Franck, T. M. *Human Rights in Third World Perspective.* Dobbs Ferry, New York: Oceana, 1982. 3 vols.
Similar in aim to the author's earlier work [488] expanded into 3 vols and including recent material. The emphasis is on civil and political rights and the material is largely drawn from the British Commonwealth, with some from the USA.

490 Gotlieb, A. E. (ed.). *Human Rights, Federalism and Minorities.* Toronto: Canadian Institute of International Affairs, 1970. 268 pp.
An important collection of papers by Canadian scholars reviewing human rights protection and procedures in Canada and in the international sphere.

491 Humana, C. (ed.). *World Human Rights Guide.* 2nd ed. London: Hodder, 1986. 368 pp.
A comparison of the levels of freedom and repression in the member states of the UN showing the extent to which each state fulfils its obligations under the Charter and the International Covenants.

492 Jaconelli, J. *Enacting a Bill of Rights: The legal problems.* London: Oxford University Press, 1980. 340 pp.
Mainly of interest to English readers, but useful in showing the difficulties arising in seeking to entrench human rights protections in a state which does not have a written constitution.

493 Kadarsky, A. *Human Rights in American and Russian Political Thought.*

Lanham, Maryland: University Press of America, 1982. 252 pp.
A major comparative study of considerable significance in the field of international relations whilst also making a major philosophical contribution to the subject.

494 Keith, K. J. (ed.). *Essays on Human Rights.* Wellington, New Zealand: Sweet and Maxwell, 1968. 199 pp.
Comparative essays on the protection of civil rights with the emphasis predominantly on New Zealand law, written to commemorate the twentieth anniversary of the Universal Declaration.

495 Koopmans, T. *Constitutional Protection of Equality.* Leiden: Sijthoff, 1975. 255 pp.
A comparative analysis of the protection afforded to the principle of equality of rights and opportunity in the USA, Canada, West Germany, France and the USSR.

496 Kramer, D. C. *Comparative Civil Rights and Liberties.* Washington: University Press of America, 1982. 381 pp.
A comparison of civil rights protection in the USA, UK, USSR, France and India.

497 Macdonald, R. St. J. and **Humphrey, J. P.** *The Practice of Freedom: Canadian essays on human rights and fundamental freedoms.* Toronto: Butterworth, 1979. 460 pp.
This collection of essays is a very useful account of the protection of human rights in Canada and is of interest to scholars concerned with the comparative protections offered.

498 Pollis, A. and **Schwab, P.** *Human Rights: Cultural and ideological perspectives.* New York: Praeger, 1979. 165 pp.
A collection of essays illustrating different perspectives on human rights. Areas reviewed include pre-revolutionary Russia, modern China, Islam and Spanish America.

499 Polyviou, P. G. *The Equal Protection of the Laws.* London: Duckworth, 1980. 759 pp.
A study of discrimination and equality under the law, principally in the USA, but with comparative reference to India and Canada.

500 Scarman, Lord. *English Law: The new dimension.* London: Stevens, 1975. 104 pp.
A distinguished English Law Lord advocates the adoption of a UK Bill of Rights along the lines of the European Convention. ·Of more interest to British readers,

but for others it is a useful account of the British constitutional position.

501 Sigler, J. A. *Minority Rights: A comparative analysis.* Westport, Connecticut: Greenwood, 1983. 245 pp.
An interesting book on the very difficult subject of minority group rights.

502 Street, H. *Freedom, the Individual and the Law.* 5th ed. London: Penguin, 1982. 328 pp.
Largely of interest to English readers, but for others perhaps the best introduction to the protection of individual freedom in England.

503 Thompson, K. W. (ed.). *The Moral Imperatives of Human Rights: A world survey.* Washington: University Press of America, 1980. 248 pp.
An important book because it touches on subjects rarely covered in Western writings. It includes chapters on human rights in the political cultures of the USSR, China, India, Africa, Islam and Latin America.

504 Van Dyke, V. *Human Rights, Ethnicity and Discrimination.* Westport, Connecticut: Greenwood, 1985. 259 pp.
A comparative study of equality and discrimination on grounds of race, language, religion, ethnicity etc., looking at experiences in Belgium, Cyprus, India, South Africa, the USA etc.

505 Veenhoven, W. A. (ed.). *Case Studies on Human Rights and Fundamental Freedoms: A world survey.* Hague: Nijhoff, 1975–6. 5 vols.
A major compilation of case studies ranging from Soviet political prisons through discrimination against Blacks and Indians in the USA to the treatment of ethnic minorities in Africa, Asia and Latin America. Few areas of the world escape notice.

Specific Rights

Rights in employment and the International Labour Organization
506 Bartolomei de la Cruz, H. G. *Protection Against Anti-Union Discrimination.* Geneva: ILO, 1976. 123 pp.
A study of the effects of laws in protecting workers against anti-union discrimination in 50 countries.

507 Caire, G. *Freedom of Association and Economic Development.* Geneva: ILO, 1977. 160 pp.
A study of industrialization in developing countries which considers whether freedom of association is an obstacle to economic development.

508 Erstling, J. A. *The Right to Organize: A survey of laws and regulations relating to the rights of workers to establish unions of their own choosing.* Geneva: ILO, 1977. 82 pp.
A review of the problems arising in connection with the right to organize.

509 Haas, E. B. *Human Rights and International Action: The case of freedom of association.* Stanford, California: Stanford University Press, 1970. 184 pp.
A controversial plea for a functional approach to the protection of human rights. Strong emphasis on the work of the ILO.

510 International Labour Office. *Freedom of Association. Digest of decisions and principles of the Committee on Freedom of Association of the Governing Body of the ILO.* 3rd ed. Geneva: ILO, 1985. 140 pp.
Digest of over 1,300 decisions reached by the ILO Committee in dealing with complaints relating to infringements of the freedom to associate.

511 International Labour Office. *The Impact of International Labour Conventions and Recommendations.* Geneva: ILO, 1976. 104 pp.
A study of the influence of international labour standards on the practice of individual countries.

512 Jenks, C. W. *Human Rights and International Labour Standards.* London: Stevens, 1960. 159 pp.
Although dated, this is still a very readable introduction to the protection of rights in employment. Needs to be read in the light of major developments occurring since it was written.

513 Jenks, C. W. *The International Protection of Trade Union Freedom.* London: Stevens, 1957. 592 pp.
A major work of its time, concerned with the developing protection of workers under international and national laws. Now somewhat out of date, but still of historical value.

514 Jenks, C. W. *Social Policy in a Changing World: The ILO response.* Geneva: International Labour Office, 1976. 265 pp.

515 Joyce, J. A. *World Labour Rights and Their Protection.* London: Croom Helm, 1980. 190 pp.
An outline of workers' rights with case studies illustrating abuse in nine different countries. A provocative and somewhat selective work.

516 Landy, E. A. *The Effectiveness of International Supervision: Thirty years of ILO experience.* London: Stevens, 1966. 268 pp.
A survey of the work and supervisory machinery of the ILO.

517 Osieke, E. *Constitutional Law and Practice in the International Labour Organization.* Hague: Nijhoff, 1985. 266 pp.

518 Shotwell, J. T. *The Origins of the International Labour Organization.* New York: Columbia University Press, 1934. 2 vols.
The most authoritative early work on the ILO.

519 Valticos, N. *International Labour Law.* Deventer, Netherlands: Kluwer, 1979. 267 pp.
A very good account of the ILO and the content of international labour law based on the more detailed *Droit International du Travail* (Paris: Dalloz, 1970) by the same author.

520 Weaver, G. L. P. *The International Labour Organization and Human Rights.* Washington: ILO, 1968. 54 pp.

Humanitarian law and the International Committee of the Red Cross
521 Bothe, M., Partsch, K. J. and **Wolf, W.** *New Rules for Victims of Armed Conflict.* Hague: Nijhoff, 1982. 746 pp.
A major study of recent developments in the protection of individuals during armed conflict.

522 Cassese, A. (ed.). *The New Humanitarian Law of Armed Conflict.* Naples: Editoriale Scientifica, 1979. 291 pp.
A collection of papers, some in English, some in French, on the Geneva Conventions of 1949 and the 1977 protocols.

523 Forsythe, D. P. *Humanitarian Politics: The International Committee of the Red Cross.* Baltimore, Maryland: Johns Hopkins University Press, 1977. 298 pp.
A scholarly monograph on the work of the International Committee of the Red Cross in developing the humanitarian law of war.

524 Hingorani, R. C. *Prisoners of War.* 2nd ed. Dobbs Ferry, New York: Oceana, 1982. 315 pp.
Not a comprehensive or authoritative textbook on the treatment of prisoners of war, but interesting as the work of an Indian scholar expressing a view of the subject from a Third World perspective.

525 Levie, H. S. *Protection of War Victims, Protocol I to the 1949 Geneva Conventions.* Dobbs Ferry, New York: Oceana, 1979–81. 4 vols.
A major compilation of the 'travaux préparatoires' of Protocol I to the Geneva Conventions. A work for the advanced scholar.

526 Macalister-Smith, P. *International Humanitarian Assistance, Disaster Relief*

Actions in International Law and Organization. Hague: Nijhoff, 1985. 260 pp.
Mainly concerned with relief actions of the UN and the Red Cross in the context
of the international provision of humanitarian support.

527 *Official Records of the Diplomatic Conference on the Re-affirmation and Development of
International Humanitarian Law Applicable in Armed Conflicts.* Buffalo, New York:
Hein, 1981. 17 vols in 9.
A major source of humanitarian law in armed conflicts.

528 Pictet, J. *Development and Principles of International Humanitarian Law.* Hague:
Nijhoff, 1985. 99 pp.
A reflection on the development and principles of international humanitarian law
by a former member of the International Committee of the Red Cross.

529 Pictet, J. (ed.). *The Geneva Conventions of 12 August 1949.* Geneva:
International Committee of the Red Cross, 1952–60. 4 vols.
A comprehensive commentary on the Conventions by one of the leading experts
in the field.

530 Pictet, J. *Humanitarian Law and the Protection of War Victims.* Leiden: Sijthoff,
1975. 152 pp.
An interesting and thought-provoking study of the law protecting non-
combatants in time of war.

531 Pictet, J. *The Principles of International Humanitarian Law.* Geneva:
International Committee of the Red Cross, 1967. 62 pp.
A short guide to the subject by one of the leading experts in the field.

532 Ronzitti, N. *Rescuing Nationals Abroad Through Military Coercion and Intervention
on Grounds of Humanity.* Dordrecht: Nijhoff, 1985. 236 pp.
An analysis of a highly sensitive and difficult issue of states which use force,
sometimes in contravention of the UN Charter, to protect their nationals abroad
or who intervene in the affairs of other states on humanitarian grounds.

533 Swinarski, C. (ed.). *Studies and Essays on International Humanitarian Law and
Red Cross Principles in Honour of Jean Pictet.* Hague: Nijhoff, 1985. 1143 pp.
A substantial and distinguished collection of papers on international humanitar-
ian law edited by the legal adviser to the International Committee of the Red
Cross.

534 Toman, K. (ed.). *Index of the Geneva Conventions for the Protection of War Victims
of 12 August 1949.* Leiden: Sijthoff, 1973. 219 pp.
Detailed indexes to the 1949 Geneva Conventions.

535 Willemin, G., Heacock, R. and **Freymond, J.** *The International Committee of the Red Cross.* Hague: Nijhoff, 1984. 209 pp.

A study of the work of the International Committee of the Red Cross in the post-war world and how it has adapted its structures and methods.

Genocide

536 Kuper, L. *Genocide: Its political use in the 20th century.* London: Penguin, 1981. 256 pp.

A sociological study of the control and prevention of genocide.

537 Kuper, L. *The Prevention of Genocide.* New Haven, Connecticut: Yale University Press, 1985. 362 pp.

Drawn from the author's earlier work and presenting a programme for the limitation and prevention of genocide.

538 Porter, J. N. (ed.). *Genocide and Human Rights: A global anthology.* Washington: University Press of America, 1982. 353 pp.

Useful essays on the broader issues of genocide and the problems faced by particular groups. A book for the general reader.

539 Ruhashyankiko, N. *Study of the Prevention and Punishment of the Crime of Genocide.* Geneva: United Nations, 1978. 186 pp.

A study of the development of the concept of genocide and measures to deal with the problem.

Self-determination, development rights and other Third World issues

540 Alexander, Y. and **Friedlander, R. A.** (eds.). *Self Determination: National regional and global dimensions.* Boulder, Colorado: Westview, 1980. 392 pp.

A valuable account of the different interpretations of the concept of self-determination with a review of the perspectives and the varying attitudes adopted toward the concept in different parts of the world.

541 Alston, P. and **Tomasevski, K.** (eds.). *The Right to Food.* Hague: Nijhoff, 1984. 228 pp.

An interesting study of economic and social aspects of human rights in respect of land tenure and the production and distribution of food.

542 Cristescu, A. *The Historical and Current Development of the Right to Self Determination on the Basis of the Charter of the United Nations and Other Instruments Adopted by the United Nations.* Geneva: United Nations, 1978. 3 vols.

A major study of the development of the right to self-determination within the framework of the UN.

543 Cristescu, A. *The Right to Self Determination. Historical and Current Developments* *on the Basis of United Nations Instruments.* New York: United Nations, 1981. 136 pp.

A useful introduction by the author of the major study in the field [542].

544 Dupuy, R.-J. (ed.). *The Right to Development at the International Level. Colloquy. The Hague, 16–18th October 1979.* Alphen aan den Rijn, Netherlands: Sijthoff and Noordhoff, 1980. 446 pp.

The text of the proceedings of a colloquium on international development law. Much of the text is in French. Contains some important discussions of the principles and difficulties of establishing development law.

545 International Commission of Jurists. *Development, Human Rights and the Rule of Law.* Oxford: Pergamon, 1981. 237 pp.

A collection of papers delivered at a conference in 1981 concerned with a wide range of economic and social development rights in the Third World. Rather political in emphasis, but provides a number of illustrations of Third World problems.

546 Johnson, H. S. *Self Determination Within the Community of Nations.* Leiden: Sijthoff, 1967. 232 pp.

A useful book on the subject written at a time when the idea of a right of self-determination was still seeking to establish itself in international affairs.

547 Okolie, C. C. *International Law Perspectives of Developing Countries: The relationship of law and economic development to basic human rights.* New York: NK, 1978. 369 pp.

A valuable Third World approach to development law.

548 Pomerance, M. *Self Determination in Law and Practice: The new doctrine in the United Nations.* Hague: Nijhoff, 1982. 154 pp.

A right-wing attack on UN practice in regard to self-determination. Contains some valid criticisms, but is more intent on making a political case against the current trends.

549 Shepherd, G. W. Jr. and **Nanda, V. P.** (eds.). *Human Rights and Third World Development.* Westport, Connecticut: Greenwood, 1985. 384 pp.

A collection of 12 essays dealing with the interrelationship of human rights and economic development.

550 Sureda, A. R. *The Evolution of the Right of Self-Determination.* Leiden: Sijthoff, 1973. 397 pp.

An important introduction to the subject largely concerned with case studies.

Rights of minorities

551 Ashworth, G. (ed.). *World Minorities.* Sunbury-on-Thames, Middlesex: Quartermaine House, 1981. 2 vols.

Together these 2 vols review the widely differing level of disadvantage suffered by minority groups. The work suffers a little from including the sillier sides of nationalism alongside the horrifying plight of the disadvantaged in countries of the Equatorial areas.

552 Ashworth, G. (ed.). *World Minorities in the Eighties.* Sunbury-on-Thames, Middlesex: Quartermaine House, 1980. 190 pp.

A companion volume to the above.

553 Lowe, M. F. *International Organization and the Protection of Minorities: Alternative approaches, prospects for the future.* Geneva: Institut Universitaire de Hautes Etudes Internationales, 1976. 219 pp.

554 McKean, W. *Equality and Discrimination Under International Law.* London: Oxford University Press, 1983. 330 pp.

A major study of the protection of minorities under post-world war peace treaties, the UN, ILO and the European Convention.

555 Lador-Lederer, J. J. *International Group Protection: Aims and methods in human rights.* Leiden: Sijthoff, 1968. 481 pp.

A major work on the protection of minority rights, albeit somewhat dated.

556 Whitaker, B. (ed.). *The Fourth World: Victims of group oppression. Eight reports from the field work of the Minority Rights Group.* New York: Schocken, 1973. 342 pp.

Eight case studies of oppression or discrimination against minority groups. Highly selective but offering important illustrations of the consequences of discrimination, sometimes extreme, sometimes subtle.

Rights of aliens, refugees etc.

557 Goodwin-Gill, G. S. *International Law and the Movement of Persons Between States.* Oxford: Clarendon Press, 1978. 324 pp.

An important study of the controls over entry into states of foreign nationals and the power of expulsion.

558 Goodwin-Gill, G. S. *The Refugee in International Law.* Oxford: Clarendon Press, 1983. 318 pp.

A major study of the degree of protection offered to refugees under international law and under the national laws of some 35 selected states.

559 Grahl-Madsen, A. *The Status of Refugees in International Law.* Leiden: Sijthoff, 1966. 2 vols.

A major theoretical and practical study of the definition and protection of refugees.

560 Grahl-Madsen, A. *Territorial Asylum.* Stockholm: Almqvist and Wiksell; Dobbs Ferry, New York: Oceana, 1980. 230 pp.
An important text on the right of asylum with a useful collection of relevant international documents.

561 Hull, E. *Without Justice For All: The constitutional rights of aliens.* London: Greenwood, 1985. 256 pp.
An examination of the way US law and public policy affects aliens within US territory. Although concerned with domestic law, it deals with issues of major international concern.

562 Kamanda, A. M. *Territorial Asylum and the Protection of Political Refugees in Public International Law.* Geneva: Carnegie Endowment, 1971. 242 pp.
A useful introduction, but somewhat dated.

563 Levy, D. M. (ed.). *Transnational Legal Problems of Refugees.* New York: Boardman, 1982. 646 pp.
A major study of the subject.

564 Lillich, R. B. *The Human Rights of Aliens in Contemporary International Law.* Manchester: Manchester University Press, 1984. 224 pp.
A valuable book on this most difficult subject.

565 Plender, R. *International Migration Law.* Leiden: Sijthoff, 1972. 339 pp.
A major study of immigration law including the position of migrant workers and refugees. Very well documented with copious reference to the national laws of states.

566 Shearer, I. A. *Extradition in International Law.* Manchester: Manchester University Press, 1971. 283 pp.
A valuable study of the controls on extradition in international and national law. Contains a great deal of comparative material.

567 Sinha, S. P. *Asylum and International Law.* Hague: Nijhoff, 1971. 366 pp.

568 United Nations, Office of the High Commissioner for Refugees. *Collection of International Legal Instruments Concerning Refugees.* 2nd ed. Geneva: United Nations, 1979. 335 pp.

569 Weis, P. *Nationality and Statelessness in International Law.* 2nd ed. Alphen aan den Rijn, Netherlands: Sijthoff and Noordhoff, 1979. 337 pp.

An important text on the determination of nationality and its consequences and the problems of statelessness.

570 Wijngaert, C. van den. *The Political Offence Exception to Extradition: The delicate problem of balancing the rights of the individual and the international public order.* Deventer, Netherlands: Kluwer, 1980. 263 pp.
A detailed account of an important and sensitive subject with valuable references to the comparative case law of several states.

Others
571 Amnesty International. *Torture in the Eighties.* London: Martin Robertson and Amnesty International, 1984. 263 pp.
A global review of the contemporary use of torture and brutal punishments throughout the world.

572 *Cultural Rights as Human Rights.* Paris: UNESCO, 1970. 125 pp.

573 Desmond, C. *Persecution East and West: Human rights, political prisoners and Amnesty.* London: Penguin, 1983. 176 pp.
A politically motivated book highlighting 'both capitalist and socialist oppression' by a controversial former Director of the British section of Amnesty International.

574 Dupuy, R. J. (ed.). *The Right to Health as a Human Right.* Alphen aan den Rijn, Netherlands: Sijthoff and Noordhoff, 1979. 500 pp.
An important book reviewing the right to an adequate standard of living, health and well-being as a human right.

575 Gormley, W. P. *Human Rights and Environment: The need for international co-operation.* Leiden: Sijthoff, 1976. 255 pp.
A thought-provoking work on an important topic, but many would doubt whether the idea of human rights should be extended into environmental matters.

576 Hevener, N. K. *International Law and the Status of Women.* Boulder, Colorado: Westview, 1982. 145 pp.
A useful compendium of texts of international instruments protecting women as a separate identifiable group in terms of employment, status etc. Includes details of treaty ratifications at the date of publication.

577 *Human Rights in Urban Areas.* Paris: UNESCO, 1983. 169 pp.
Analysis of the obstacles to the implementation of human rights in urban areas.

578 *Human Rights of Population Programmes with Special Reference to Human Rights Law.* Paris: UNESCO, 1977. 154 pp.

579 International Commission of Jurists. *Legal Protection of Privacy: A comparative survey of ten countries.* Geneva: ICJ, 1972. 212 pp.
Discusses the nature of privacy and its protection in 10 selected countries.

580 Khushalani, Y. *Dignity and Honour of Women as Basic and Fundamental Rights.* Hague: Nijhoff, 1982. 154 pp.
A plea for the special protection of women as part of the developing law of human rights.

581 Middleton, K. and **Mersky, R. M.** *Freedom of Expression: A collection of best writings.* Buffalo, New York: Hein, 1981. 504 pp.
A collection of writings published over the previous thirty years on the fundamental right of freedom of expression.

582 Ramcharan, B. G. (ed.). *The Right to Life in International Law.* Hague: Nijhoff, 1985. 382 pp.
A collection of essays by a number of contributors from a wide range of disciplines on different aspects of the right to life under contemporary international and regional instruments.

583 Robertson, A. H. *Privacy and Human Rights.* Manchester: Manchester University Press, 1973. 497 pp.
A collection of papers given at a conference on the European Convention in 1970. Still interesting although the reader needs to be aware of the major developments in European jurisprudence which have taken place since that time.

584 Santa Cruz, H. *Racial Discrimination.* New York: United Nations, 1976. 284 pp.
A revised and updated version of a study on racial discrimination in the political, economic, social and cultural spheres.

585 Stromholm, S. *Rights of Privacy and Rights of the Personality: A comparative study.* Stockholm: Norstadt, 1967. 250 pp.
A useful comparative study of the protection of rights of privacy in German, French and Scandinavian laws.

13   Other Works of Reference

Guides to Theses

The guides to theses and research work in progress listed here enable the scholar to access advanced human rights research which may not be readily available elsewhere in printed form. As their titles suggest, most of these guides cover the whole range of academic research and not merely legal studies. However, on the whole, they are fully indexed and should provide ready access to relevant work.

586 *Comprehensive Dissertation Index, 1861–1972.* Ann Arbor, Michigan: University Microfilms, 1973. 37 vols with supplements.

587 *Dissertation Abstracts International.* Ann Arbor, Michigan: University Microfilms, 1938–. Monthly.

588 *Index to Theses Accepted for Higher Degrees in the Universities of Great Britain and Ireland and the Council for National Academic Awards, 1950 to date.* London: Aslib, 1953–. Twice yearly.

589 Reynolds, M. M. *A Guide to Theses and Dissertations: An annotated bibliography of bibliographies.* Detroit: Gale, 1975. 599 pp.

590 *Current Research in Britain.* Boston Spa, West Yorkshire: British Library, 1985. 4 vols.
National register of current research in British universities and colleges. Replaces *Research in British Universities, Polytechnics and Colleges.* The Social Science volume lists a number of relevant projects.

Human Rights Dictionaries

This list is confined to those glossaries which are particularly related to human rights terminology. There are a number of general legal glossaries which provide translations of ordinary legal terminology. Similarly, a large number of legal dictionaries provide definitions of basic legal terms.

591 Doucet, M. *Dictionary of Human Rights: Spanish, English, French.* Paris: La Maison du Dictionnaire, 1980. 2 vols.

592 European Parliament. *Terminology of Human Rights.* Strasbourg: European Parliament, 1977. 313 pp.
Entries in Danish, Dutch, English, French, German and Italian.

593 *Human Rights Thesaurus: Working Tool.* London: Human Rights International Documentation System, 1982. 82 pp.

594 *International Labour Organization. ILO Thesaurus: Labour, employment and training terminology.* 2nd ed. Geneva: ILO, 1978. 223 pp.

595 Marie, J. B. *Glossaire des Droits de l'Homme. Glossary of Human Rights. English–French.* Paris: Editions de la Maison des Sciences de l'Homme, 1981. 339 pp.
Published under the auspices of the International Institute of Human Rights, this is one of the main guides to the basic terms of the subject as they appear in the main international and regional instruments.

596 Paenson, I. *et al. Manual of the Terminology of Public International Law (Law of Peace) and International Organizations.* Brussels: Bruylant, 1983. 846 pp.
Entries in English, French, Russian and Spanish.

597 United Nations. *Human Rights: Legal, social and administrative terms.* Geneva: United Nations, 1981. 282 pp.

Directories and Other Reference Books

598 Akey, D. *Encylopedia of Associations.* 18th ed. Detroit: Gale, 1984. 4 vols. Annual.
Mainly concerned with US bodies, but Vol. 4 lists international organizations based outside the USA and the work includes reference to a number of groups which are interested in human rights matters.

599 Atherton, A. L. *International Organizations: A guide to information sources.* Detroit: Gale, 1976. 350 pp.

600 *Directory of British Associations and Associations in Ireland.* Ed. G. P. Henderson and S. P. A. Henderson. 8th ed. Beckenham, Kent: CBD Research, 1986. 506 pp.

Provides basic information about a large number of British associations, groups being arranged alphabetically with a subject index. A few organizations concerned with human rights are listed. A companion volume deals with Councils, Committees and Boards and an associated volume deals with European organizations, although few of those listed are relevant in this area of research.

601 Garling, M. *The Human Rights Handbook: A guide to British and American international human rights organizations.* London: Macmillan, 1979. 299 pp.

A useful directory of voluntary and professional organizations concerned with human rights. Many organizations listed here are based in the UK, but the volume also includes a selection of major US and international groups. For each organization, basic factual information is provided along with a general survey of the group's work. The volume includes reference to a variety of 'single issue' groups which are not listed here. The researcher should, however, note that in the years since publication some of the information given, particularly as regards addresses, has become outdated.

602 *Human Rights Organizations and Periodicals Directory.* Berkeley, California: Meiklejohn Civil Liberties Institute, 1973–. Irregular.

A fifth edition, produced by David Christiano and Lisa Young, is in preparation.

603 *Research Centers Directory.* Detroit: Gale Research, 1960–. Irregular.

'A guide to university related and other non-profit research organizations carrying on continuing research programmes.' Covers all subject areas.

604 Wiseberg, L. and **Scoble, H. M.** *Human Rights Directory: Latin America, Africa, Asia.* Washington: Human Rights Internet, 1981. 244 pp.

Lists over 400 organizations in the Third World. See also [605 and 606].

605 Wiseberg, L. and **Sirett, H.** (eds.). *Human Rights Directory: Western Europe.* Washington: Human Rights Internet, 1982. 334 pp.

Lists around 1,000 organizations based in Western Europe. See also [604 and 606].

606 Wiseberg, L. and **Sirett, H.** (eds.). *North American Human Rights Directory.* 3rd ed. Washington: Human Rights Internet, 1984. 264 pp.

Revised edition of *Human Rights Directory* which first appeared in 1979. A further volume covering Eastern Europe is due to appear. See also [604 and 605].

These three volumes provide the fullest listing of organizations concerned with the protection of human rights both at the national and the international level. Inevitably many of the bodies listed are only of transitory interest, being set up to deal with particular human rights issues, whilst, as the authors point out, a few groups may not justify their inclusion at all. Nevertheless, the directories provide a vast amount of information for groups from all parts of the world, ranging from brief factual details to summaries of their activities. The North American directory is now in its third edition, thereby avoiding problems of currency, although with groups of this nature changes of personnel and location are bound to occur. The directories are supplemented by information contained in the *Human Rights Internet Reporter* [263].

607 *Yearbook of International Organizations.* Munich: Saur, 1948–. 3 vols. Biennial. Probably the fullest available general listing on international organizations in all spheres, coverage ranging from inter-governmental organizations to informal pressure groups. Vol. 1 provides basic details on organizations, including names, addresses, personnel, areas of special concern, etc., Vol. 2 provides details of national membership of particular groups. Vol. 3 provides a classified directory of organizations by subject and region.

Other works which are particularly suited for reference use, notably those by Humana [491] and Osmanczyk [381], are noted in the chapter on monographs. The following guides to library holdings should also be noted.

608 Garling, M. *Human Rights Research Guide. Library Holdings in London on Human Rights, Censorship and Freedom of Expression.* London: Writers and Scholars Educational Trust, 1978. 77 pp.
Now a little outdated.

609 Lewanski, R. C. *Subject Collections in European Libraries.* 2nd ed. London: Bowker, 1978. 495 pp.

610 *World Guide to Libraries. Internationales Bibliothekshandbuch.* 6th ed. Munich: Saur, 1983. 1,218 pp.
Helga Lengenfelder, the editor, has also produced a guide to special libraries.

PART III

List of selected organizations

List of Selected Organizations

In Part III of this *Keyguide* are listed selected human rights organizations. International and regional inter-governmental organizations are listed first, but a selection of important non-governmental organizations which concern themselves with human rights is also included. There are large numbers of such bodies, but here emphasis is on those which operate throughout the world rather than those which are primarily concerned with particular issues within their own country. Within this selection there will undoubtedly be some omissions of important groups and readers are referred to other more comprehensive directories, such as the regional guides produced by Human Rights Internet [604–606], and Garling's *Human Rights Handbook* [601], although some of the latter's information is now outdated. These guides contain far more information about particular organizations, and the Human Rights Internet publications are particularly valuable in their detailing of human rights groups operating within individual countries.

Other more general directories may be used to supplement and update the information given here. For example, the CBD Directories of European and British Associations may be found useful, although their coverage is somewhat patchy. This is to some extent inevitable given the ephemeral and transitory nature of many groupings working in the field of human rights.

The information given here for each organization comprises its name and address and, generally, a brief note of its objectives, where these relate to the protection of human rights, alongside a list of the major publications emanating from the body.

Inter-governmental Organizations

611 Council of Europe
67006 Strasbourg, France

Responsible for many publications dealing with human rights in Europe. The main series are detailed in Part II [198–220]. See also European Commission of Human Rights and European Court of Human Rights [612].

612 European Commission of Human Rights. European Court of Human Rights
Council of Europe, 67006 Strasbourg Cedex, France

The Directorate of Human Rights produces a wide range of documentation which is available to individuals on request. Items available include press releases, minutes, reports of the Commission in so far as they have been made public, and an annual survey of activities. These can be obtained from the Directorate at the above address. Other sales publications such as the series of Decisions and Reports can be obtained from the Publications Section at the same address. Further information on documentation emanating from the Commission and Court can be found in Part II [198–220].

613 European Community
Office for Official Publications of the European Communities, 6 Rue de Commerce, 2985 Luxembourg

Although not directly concerned with human rights, certain areas of community activity do impinge on the subject, as for example in the free movement of labour. Official documentation in the form of directives and regulations can be obtained from the above address, as can a whole range of secondary material.

614 Inter-American Commission on Human Rights. Organization of American States
1899 F Street NW, 8th Floor, Washington, D.C. 20006, USA

A range of publications both in Spanish and English can be obtained from the Organization. See Part II [221–231].

615 Inter-American Court of Human Rights of the Organization of American States
Apartado 6906, San José, Costa Rica

Details of publications emanating from the IACHR can be found in Part II [221–231].

616 International Committee of the Red Cross
17 Avenue de la Paix, 1211 Geneva, Switzerland

Of major importance for its work in the field of humanitarian law, some of the major publications of the Committee in the field are listed in Part II [195–197].

617 International Labour Organization
4 Route des Morillons, 1211 Geneva 22, Switzerland
London office: 96/98 Marsham Street, London SW1P 4LY, England
Produces a wide range of documentation ranging from free literature available on request to those series and studies listed in Part II [182–194].

618 League of Arab States
37 Avenue Khereddine Pacha, Tunis, Tunisia
The Permanent Committee for Human Rights operates within the Legal Affairs Department of the League and may be able to provide useful information.

619 Organization of African Unity
PO Box 3243, Addis Ababa, Ethiopia
Can provide details of the African Charter and its documentation.

620 Organization of American States
Dept of Public Information, 19th and Constitution Avenue NW, Washington, DC 20006, USA
See also the entries for the Inter-American Commission on Human Rights [614] and Inter-American Court of Human Rights [615]. Relevant publications are listed in Part II [221–231].

621 Organization of the Islamic Conference
Kilo 6, Mecca Road, PO Box 178, Jeddah, Saudi Arabia
There is little documentation in English relating to the Islamic protection of human rights, but this body and the League of Arab States [618] may be able to provide information.

622 United Nations
777 United Nations Plaza, New York, NY 10017, USA, and also Palais des Nations, 1211 Geneva, Switzerland
Although the UN produces a vast range of relevant documentation, some of which is listed in Part II [138–174], the interested student may also wish to approach the various subsidiary UN bodies concerned with particular human rights and a few of these are listed here.

623 United Nations Commission on Human Rights
addresses as [622]
Established under the auspices of ECOSOC and directly concerned with the drafting and implementation of international human rights provisions. Some, but not all, of the work is made public through annual reports and documentation. See [159].

624 United Nations Committee on the Elimination of Racial Discrimination
addresses as [622]
Produces sessional reports which go to the General Assembly.

625 United Nations Division of Human Rights
   addresses as [622]
Secretariat for the Commission on Human Rights and its sub-commission. Responsible for a range of documentation, including the *Yearbook* [170] and the *Bulletin* [151].

626 United Nations Economic and Social Council
   addresses as [622]
The parent organization for the Commission on Human Rights. See [152].

627 United Nations Educational Scientific and Cultural Organization. Division of Human Rights and Peace
   7 Place de Fontenoy, 75700 Paris, France
See Part II [175–181] for details of publications.

628 United Nations High Commission for Refugees
   Centre William Rappard, 154 Rue de Lausanne, 1202 Geneva, Switzerland
See [150].

629 United Nations Sub Commission on the Prevention of Discrimination and the Protection of Minorities
   777 United Nations Plaza, New York, NY 10017, USA
A sub-commission of the Commission on Human Rights [622], to which body it makes periodic reports. See [165].

630 World Health Organization
   1211 Geneva 27, Switzerland
A specialized agency of the UN which produces some relevant documentation.

Non-governmental Organizations

631 Americas Watch
   165 East 56th Street, New York, NY 10022, USA
Concerned with rights in the Americas.

632 Amnesty International (British Section)
   5 Roberts Place (off Bowling Green Lane), London EC1 OEJ, England

633 Amnesty International, International Secretariat
   1 Easton Street, London WC1X 8DJ, England

634 Amnesty International (USA)
   304 West 58th Street, New York, NY 10019, USA
Amnesty International is the leading non-governmental organization operating

in the field of human rights, with branches throughout the world, although only three addresses are listed here. The organization has produced a large number of reports on human rights violations throughout the world and is also responsible for a number of serial publications which may be of interest to the researcher. Particular mention should be made of the annual report produced by the organization summarizing its recent activity, the *Amnesty International Newsletter* appearing monthly, and the *Amnesty Journal* appearing six times a year. Other serial publications include *Matchbox* and *Amnesty Action*. These publications may be obtained from the addresses listed above, but it should also be noted that a mass of Amnesty documentation is available on microfiche from the Inter-Documentation Company, Zug, Switzerland.

635 Anti-Apartheid Movement
13 Mandela Street, London NW1 ODW, England

Although organizations which are concerned with human rights violations in a particular country are not generally listed, the work of the Anti-Apartheid movement is of particular note at the present time. Amongst other publications the group produces the monthly *Anti-Apartheid News*.

636 Anti-Slavery Society for the Protection of Human Rights
180 Brixton Road, London SW9 6AT, England

The group has a long and honourable history for its fight against slavery and the exploitation of forced labour. The *Anti-Slavery Reporter* appears annually and the group also produces a newsletter.

637 British Institute of Human Rights
Faculty of Laws, King's College, Strand, London WC2, England

The Institute is currently in the process of reorganization, but is generally responsible for a range of research into legal aspects of human rights issues particularly in the European context. The group has produced a number of reports and was involved with the *Human Rights Review* [267] which appeared until 1981.

638 Centre for Human Rights and Responsibilities
16 Ponsonby Place, London SW1, England

Associated with the Fédération Internationale des Droits de l'Homme [640].

639 European Human Rights Foundation
95A Chancery Lane, London WC2A 1DT, England

640 Fédération Internationale des Droits de l'Homme
27 Rue Jean-Dolent, 75014 Paris, France

A federation composed of nationally based affiliates in over 30 countries. The group is concerned with rights violations throughout the world and has produced a number of valuable reports. The weekly *Lettre de la F.I.D.H.* comments on recent events in the field.

641 Freedom House
20 West 40th Street, New York, NY 10018, USA

A body concerned with civil and political freedoms. Freedom House produces a number of relevant surveys including *Freedom Appeals, Freedom at Issue* and *Freedom in the World* [259].

642 Human Rights Internet
1502 Ogden Street NW, Washington, DC 20010, USA

Described as an international communications centre and clearing house for human rights information. The group is involved in a large number of information-gathering and disseminating activities. Publications emanating from the group include the invaluable *Human Rights Internet Reporter* [263] and various directories [604–606]. In addition, a range of non-governmental documentation from many sources collected by Human Rights Internet is available on microfiche from the Inter-Documentation Company, Zug, Switzerland.

643 Human Rights Network
c/o National Council of Social Services, 26 Bedford Square, London WC1B 3HU, England

A body which seeks to encourage the exchange of information between organizations concerned with human rights. The group maintains a useful file of groups with their contact points.

644 HURIDOCS. Human Rights Information and Documentation System
Nieuwe Gracht 94, 3512 LX Utrecht, Netherlands

A specialist body which is seeking to improve the standards of documentation and information provision by groups which are concerned with human rights. Publishes *HURIDOCS News* and other surveys including a useful bibliography of new publications in the field covering the period 1970–81. See also [419].

645 Index on Censorship
See Writers and Scholars International [663].

646 Inter-Parliamentary Union
Place de Petit Saconnex, 1209 Geneva 28, Switzerland

A quasi-official organization with its own statutes and secretariat. The organization considers the human rights record of individual countries as part of its general activity and has produced reports on rights violations in various South American countries over the past few years.

647 Interights. International Centre for the Legal Protection of Human Rights
Kingsway Chambers, 46 Kingsway, London WC2B 6EN, England

Produces *Interights Bulletin* [271].

648 International Association of Democratic Lawyers
49 Avenue Jupiter, 1190 Brussels, Belgium
Concerned with all aspects of human rights, the group formerly produced a bulletin *Review of Contemporary Law/Revue De Droit Contemporain* which contained some relevant material.

649 International Commission of Jurists
PO Box 120, 109 Route de Chene, 1224 Chene Bougeries, Geneva, Switzerland
One of the most important non-governmental organizations working in the field of human rights, the Commission enjoys consultative status with the UN, UNESCO and the Council of Europe. It has produced many useful studies and is also responsible for the *ICJ Review* [273] and a newsletter.

650 International Documentation and Communication Center
Via S. Maria dell'Anima 30, 00186 Rome, Italy
Maintains a file of documentation relating to human rights protection, particularly in the Third World.

651 International Federation for Human Rights
See Fédération Internationale des Droits de l'Homme [640].

652 International Human Rights Law Group
1346 Connecticut Avenue NW, Suite 502, Washington, DC 20036, USA

653 International Institute of Human Rights
1 Quai Lezay Marnesia, 67000 Strasbourg, France
Concerned with research in the field of human rights, the training of teachers, and the general improvement of public awareness of the subject. A range of publications is produced, notably the *Human Rights Law Journal* [265] which is produced under the auspices of the organization.

654 International League for Human Rights
777 United Nations Plaza, Suite 6F, New York, NY 10017, USA or 236 East 46th Street, New York, NY 10017, USA
Research into all aspects of human rights. The group produces an annual review and a *Human Rights Bulletin* [262].

655 International Peace Information Service
Kerstraat 150, 2000 Antwerp, Belgium
A subsidiary of Pax Christi International which collects documentation relating to human rights protection in Europe.

656 Lelio Basso International Foundation for the Rights and Liberations of Peoples
Via Dogana Vecchia 5, Rome 00186, Italy

A new group which has produced several useful studies.

657 Ligue des Droits de l'Homme, League for Human Rights
27 Rue Jean Dolent, 75014 Paris, France

One of the oldest human rights organizations concerned with rights both in France and worldwide. Publishes a bi-monthly journal *Hommes et Libertés*.

658 Minority Rights Group
Benjamin Franklin House, 29 Craven Street, London WC2N 5NT, England

Research on a whole range of human rights violations in so far as they affect minorities of any sort. A series of useful studies has been published.

659 Survival International
Benjamin Franklin House, 29 Craven Street, London WC2N 5NT, England, and also 2121 Decatur Place NW, Washington, DC 20008, USA

Concerned with the rights of indigenous peoples and other minorities. Publishes an annual review, quarterly newsletter and other documentation including bulletins and press releases.

660 United Nations Association
3 Whitehall Court, London SW1A 2EL, England, and also 300 East 42nd Street, New York 10017, USA

Deals with human rights questions as one aspect of UN activity. Articles on the subject appear in the Association's newspaper *New World*. The Association also produces occasional human rights briefings.

661 World Federation of United Nations Associations
Centre International, 3 Rue de Varembe, CP 54, 1211 Geneva 20, Switzerland

662 World Peace Through Law Center
1000 Connecticut Avenue NW, Suite 800, Washington, DC 20036, USA

Concerned with all aspects of human rights.

663 Writers and Scholars International
39C Highbury Place, London N5 1QP, England

Concerned with freedom of expression, produces the *Index on Censorship* [268].

Index

The index is a single alphabetical sequence of authors, titles, subjects and organizations. All publications and organizations listed in Parts II and III are included here, with the exception of a few *Annual Reports* and other such publications issued by corporate bodies. Also included are important topics and sources of information discussed in Part I, although the indexing of this part is not exhaustive. All works are listed under title and, where appropriate, also under author, editor or corporate body. The arrangement is word by word with abbreviations and acronyms treated as single words. Numbers without brackets refer to page numbers within the volume; numbers within brackets refer to item numbers in Parts II and III.